Launch with God

Launch with God

How to Build a Business
That Matters and Live Out
Your God-Given Purpose

Zach Windahl

COPYRIGHT © 2021 ZACH WINDAHL
All rights reserved.

LAUNCH WITH GOD
How to Build a Business That Matters and Live Out Your God-Given Purpose

ISBN   978-1-5445-2324-8   Paperback
         978-1-5445-2323-1   Ebook

To my parents, Pete and T. Windahl.

Your never-ending prayers made all of this happen.

Also, thanks for showing me how to chase my dreams
with wisdom instead of emotion.
That's a game changer.

Contents

Introduction

I threw myself a party. We're talking a fancy, five-course-meal-type party at one of my favorite restaurants in Minneapolis, Bellecour, which I actually helped open a few years prior.

I booked the Garden Room—a light, airy space with French doors that opened out into well-tended greenery and a marble water fountain. It was classy-classy.

Everyone I cared about was there: my parents, my friends, and all of my coworkers at The Brand Sunday, a company I had founded two years before and grown while working full-time in sales.

The dinner was a celebration, a culmination of years of work. I was finally leaving my corporate job to work full-time at The Brand Sunday. To reach this point, I had gone years without a day off.

I had missed out on nights with friends,

holidays,

unforgettable trips,

and a thousand lazy Saturdays.

Finally, it was all paying off.

But this moment was bigger than that. Like many Christian entrepreneurs, I had always felt my God-given purpose in life was to create not just a successful business but a successful business that *mattered*.

This moment was to announce that I'd finally done it.

As our dinner of black truffle fondue called pommes de terre dauphine, French onion soup, and sweet corn agnolotti (aka the best pasta I've ever had in my life) concluded, I toasted each person in turn, letting them know what they meant to me, and this moment.

To my parents, for being such great sources of inspiration over the years and pushing me to pursue my dreams.

To Caleb and Ethan, for being my best friends and always encouraging every one of my crazy ideas.

To the Activ team, for helping me take the business to levels I never expected.

To the Tristan fulfillment team, for believing in our first project and pivoting as things took off.

It didn't take long for me to break down in tears of gratitude for all these people had helped me accomplish. It was because they believed in me that I was able to live out my dreams. And that hit me deep.

Don't get me wrong. I knew the road ahead wasn't going to be easy. I knew firsthand that 90 percent of businesses fail (four of mine already had), and I would have to double my efforts to make sure that didn't happen at The Brand Sunday. The hard path was only going to get harder. The safety net was gone. There was no other job, no alternative career left.

This was it. It was all on me, yet I felt neither fearful nor alone. I knew I had God with me in this, and with God as my partner, I knew we would be a success.

GOD REALLY IS EVERYWHERE

If you haven't read the book that launched my entrepreneurial career, *The Bible Study*, no worries. If you've never made it all the way through the Bible, that's okay too. In fact, just so we're all starting on the same page, let me condense God's Word down for you to just two commandments:

1. Love God with all of your heart, soul, mind, and strength.

2. Love your neighbor.

That's it—or at least, that's at the root of it.

What those commandments mean in practice is that we have to love God first. Then, we have to extend that love to each other. Love should inspire how we interact with family and friends. When we meet a stranger, we should meet them with love. When we consider big life decisions, we have to consider them through the prism of love.

And God always has to be at the center of everything we do.

And I mean everything.

It's funny how Christians implicitly reject this idea by breaking up their lives into separate categories. This bit is spiritual; this bit is secular.

Church: spiritual

Sports: secular

Charity: spiritual

Wellness: secular

Prayer: spiritual

Work: secular

The only time work makes its way into the spiritual column is when someone goes into a field directly connected to the Bible, usually as a pastor or missionary. Those are absolutely valuable, spiritual jobs. But you know what else is a spiritual job?

Making shoes.

At least, that's the case according to Martin Luther (or one of his followers...there's a bit of a debate about who said this, but the point stands!). As Luther put it, the shoemaker's work is spiritual because "God is interested in good craftsmanship."

Here's a crazy truth for you: there's no such thing as "secular." Everything God has touched—so, everything—is spiritual.

Our whole lives belong to God, and God works through us in every part of our lives.

And that includes business—especially business. God actually thrives on business and the creation of business, so long as that business is designed to *matter*.

GOD IS IN BUSINESS

I remember when I realized that I wasn't called to be a pastor. Up until then, I saw all of these "celebrity pastors" crushing it in the name of Jesus, which I thought was so cool, as a potential future. But deep down I knew that wasn't for me. Truthfully, I just wanted to feel a sense of purpose in testifying to God's greatness every day.

My interest had less to do with developing a sermon every week and more to do with creating something that mattered. It took me a long time to realize that it wasn't the job title that matters; it's how you do the job. Remember Luther's words.

And you can be a good craftsman in any career.

An artist can be a good craftsman, as can an engineer, a nurse, a football coach, or a teacher. Even when people accept this, though, for some reason, a line is always drawn at business.

Business is seen as entirely, uncompromisingly secular.

That's just not the case. If you were made to be an entrepreneur, that doesn't mean you were made to work in the secular world, it means you have to make entrepreneurship spiritual.

And to be spiritual, you have to, once again:

1. Love God with all of your heart, soul, mind, and strength.

2. Love your neighbor.

So you can create a clothing line *and* help clothe the homeless. You can open a café *and* use fair trade beans that ensure everyone involved gets paid enough to live a good life. You can run a recording studio *and* concentrate on putting out positive music that improves people's lives.

In other words, your business has to put God first and focus around loving your neighbor.

You don't have to be a pastor or a missionary to work for God. In fact, you don't even have to explicitly make your business Christian.

If you're a baker, you don't have to put a cross on every croissant.

If you're a clothing designer, you don't have to print Scripture on every shirt.

There's nothing wrong with those choices—the problem is they're so...

limiting.

This is the God of the whole universe we're talking about here— God of the heavens and the earth, the seas and the land, and all the creatures on it. You don't think He can partner with you if you just want to make the best pastries in town? Of course He can. Luther thought so too. According to him, the shoemaker works alongside God "not by putting little crosses on the shoes but by making good shoes."

By advancing God's commandments to love Him and put Him first, you advance the Kingdom in the best way you can. More than that, you advance the Kingdom in the way you were *designed to do it*.

A cake that brings people joy and happiness advances the Kingdom.

A clothing line that uses an environmentally friendly supply chain and donates extra materials to the poor advances the Kingdom.

So does a business that uses fair trade products and pays a living wage to employees.

That is all Kingdom work. God gave us all purpose, and He made us all different.

We aren't all destined to be pastors, but we are all destined to follow Him and serve Him.

If you were created to be an entrepreneur, that is what you should be. The point is to make sure that whatever business you build *matters*, and it matters by advancing God's story and His Kingdom. It helps feed and clothe the poor, gives people dignity, reduces suffering, protects the planet, enriches your community, or simply makes people happy in a wholesome way.

That's God's purpose in action—and you can be part of it.

THE STAKES ARE HIGH

One of the most attractive things about being part of the Church, I think, is that you are so clearly aligned with the heart of God. Through you, God offers the potential for eternal life. Through you, God presents His story to people. That's consequential...to say the least.

But while the Church is obviously God's first consideration, business is not necessarily secondary. Have you ever noticed how people in the Bible are always working?

They're building ships or building tents.

They're shepherds and fishermen.

God's Son was a professional carpenter.

The first man He created was a gardener.

Sure, He also works through priests like Aaron, but most of the biggest players in His story have been hard workers.

You might even call them entrepreneurs.

A small business is never small in the eyes of God. To Him, it is a great event if it follows His commandments. As Mother Teresa once said, "Not all of us can do great things, but we can do small things with great love."

And to God, a small thing done with great love *is* a great thing.

When you look at it that way, it sounds like that business idea you have is pretty important...

on a cosmic level.

It may only be a bookshop to you, but to God, it's a part of the work He will lay down that leads to His Kingdom. At least, if that bookshop matters and operates by the tenets of God's Word. God is pretty clear on this in Proverbs 11:26: "The people curse him who holds back grain, but a blessing is on the head of him who sells it."

Or as the Passion Translation updates it: "People will curse the businessman with no ethics, but the one with a social conscience receives praise from all" (TPT).

So if you feel you were born to be a Christian *and* a business-person, you absolutely can be—and you'll be advancing the Kingdom even as you become a success. But only if you do this the right way.

GETTING FROM HERE TO THERE

If you're like me, all of this sounds good. But it can also sound nearly impossible. Starting a small business can feel abso-lutely overwhelming—let alone one that has a part to play in the cosmic pursuit of God's purpose in the world.

Where do you even start?

And how do you make sure you're bringing God along?

These are not easy questions to answer, and unfortunately, there are not a lot of resources out there that tackle both questions.

That's what this book is for.

It is not a deep dive into Scripture.

It's not a get-rich-quick plan that is all about building your empire.

It's also not a book that will show you what business you should develop.

Instead, this is a book for people who feel their God-given purpose is in entrepreneurship. If that's you, the pages ahead will provide you with a framework to launch a profitable business that matters.

As a Christian, you have access to heavenly resources to help you fulfill your purpose. God listens, and He responds. God guides, and He nurtures. But this is not a one-way conversation. You have to do your part as well.

That requires you to take an active role here.

Ahead, we'll see where you fit into God's story and how you can take that sense of purpose and clarify a direction that leads to fulfilling it. Then, we'll look at the tools you need to overcome the early obstacles to moving into business before we take on the real world, and how you find and develop that Big Idea that makes all the difference.

We'll walk through what it takes to launch that idea, and then we'll look ahead at what it means to be a successful Christian business owner.

That way, we can get to the core of what it takes to create a business in partnership with God.

If you do this right, you'll experience the joy of walking in the freedom of your calling and living up to your God-given potential. All because you'll have built something that matters—to you, to your community, and to God.

Success may not necessarily look the way you imagine it or come on your timetable, but it will arrive in its way and in its time because you and your entrepreneurial purpose are part of God's plan.

God has a stake in your success. You are under His blessing. Earning that blessing is up to you.

And it starts by recognizing the place your business idea has in His story.

Part I

Partnering with God

1

God Is Creative

I set the goal of being a millionaire by age twenty-six.

Instead, I was hitting rock bottom.

I had abandoned my clothing brand after it didn't take off as expected. The TV show I had been working on hadn't been picked up by a network. And the new owners who had taken over the restaurant I had been working at had fired me along with the rest of the staff.

Bummer.

Instead of moving into my first mansion, I was moving back in with my parents.

Sitting alone in my car parked outside of Starbucks on an appropriately rainy night, I realized I had no direction and no purpose in my life. I knew I was meant to be an entrepreneur—it's all I'd ever wanted to be—but I seemed incapable of making any headway. I felt like it was all over. I'd built my life around the assumption that success meant making money and being my own boss, and here I was, unemployed with barely a dollar to my name.

I worked for six years without a day off, only to see each dream fail. After so much disappointment, I was ready to call it quits—on my dreams and on my purpose.

But before I did, I decided I needed to talk with God first. I'd always been a believer, but if I was honest, I hadn't really considered God much in my pursuit of success. It had always been about what *I* wanted. In my moment of despair, I called out to Him:

"Okay, God, I know I've been selfish. I know I haven't always put You first. So I'm going to give You two years of my life. I'll put You first in everything. You guide the way. You call the shots. But after that, if I find myself back here, I'm done. I'm giving up on my faith."

LESSONS FROM THE GARDEN

The first thing I did when I decided to re-dedicate my life to God was start reading the Bible—and I mean *really* read it. If I was going to give myself over to God, I needed to know what He was all about. So instead of searching for the famous passages or a good verse to memorize, I decided to read the book. All of it. Genesis to Revelation. In ninety days.

As soon as I started, I was blown away—on page one! In fact, my first lesson was in the first line I read: "In the beginning, God *created* the heavens and the earth."

I've heard that line so often, I suppose I never really thought about it. God, it turned out, was creative. I had spent my whole career trying to *create* a business where I could *be creative*—designing shirts, recording music, writing books—and all that time, I was expressing the most God-like quality of them all.

There is nothing more God-like than trying to put order and design into chaos.

When God created our world, He took something that was "worthless"—another translation of the Hebrew word *tohu* that we often see as "void"—and crafted it into something valuable.

He created something that enabled life to flourish.

And just think of how it has flourished.

God's creative energy is visible in everything: the diverse beauty of the animal kingdom, the tranquility of nature, the perfection of the laws of the universe from gravity to the forces that hold atoms together, the majesty of the stars—and all the materials He left us to create the world we live in.

The more I read, the more I realized He's also a pretty decent author.

WORK IS WORSHIP

That was all in the first two verses. Reading on just a bit further, I discovered another very important fact about existence:

God made us to work—and that work is meant to be creative.

Genesis 2:15 says, "Then the LORD God took the man and put him in the garden of Eden to *abad* it and keep it."

We often translate *abad* as "cultivate" here, but that misses all the nuance in the word. *Abad* isn't just about gardening, it incorporates the whole world of work, worship, and craftsmanship. In other words, the very first thing God wanted us to do—as soon as we were created—was worship Him in the form of work.

And right away, He set work tasks before us. Within a few verses, He presented Adam with all the animals and birds in creation so that Adam could name them. The way Adam cultivated went beyond tending the Garden, it involved sharing in the creative process *with God*.

Adam is God's partner in building the world. That's how God designed things to work in the perfection of the Garden.

This isn't just some story we're supposed to glance over on the way to the commandments or the prophets or the Gospels. God has placed this lesson *first* in the Bible. It's the *first thing* you learn about Him, His world, and our place in it. He did this to show how He wants us to interact with Him and the world.

This is the ideal: to change the world in partnership with God in order to give value to His creation.

Giving value to the world through new creation...

Is there any better description of an entrepreneur?

GOD'S STORY IS FULL OF ENTREPRENEURS

Adam isn't our only entrepreneur in the Bible. In fact, God seeking out entrepreneurs to help us return to grace is a huge part of God's story!

Further along in Genesis, we meet Noah, a man enterprising enough to literally build a boat large enough to save existence before the flood arrives.

Later, we find Joseph, who moves God's story forward by pursuing a career as a freelance dream interpreter for people in high power. That's a career Daniel will later follow.

In Exodus, after God delivers the Israelites from Egypt, He has Moses seek out a craftsman named Bezalel to build the Ark of the Covenant so He can reside with His people.

David is a musician who, like Joseph, finds a place at the height of society because of his artistic skill.

Entrepreneurship isn't limited to Old Testament figures, either.

The Son of God Himself was a carpenter.

Paul, the apostle who spread the Word to the world, worked as a traveling tentmaker—essentially running a small business to fund his efforts to share the gospel.

In each of these cases, God partnered with creative, entrepreneurial individuals to guide humanity back to Him.

Time after time, God's story is about entrepreneurs working with God to deliver us to Him. This was His plan in every story in the Bible—from Adam to Paul. And this is how we fit into His story today.

GOD'S STORY CONTINUES TODAY

There's a temptation to believe that God's story is finished. After all, the Bible is complete. It goes from "In the beginning" to "The grace of the Lord Jesus Christ be with all. Amen" at the end of

Revelation. The story takes us from creation and the fall through to redemption in Jesus Christ and as far as the end of time.

If we think about God's story as existing between book covers, we get the sense that we're just meant to hang about and wait around: accept Jesus, go to church, and wait until God chooses a time to start the fireworks.

But God's story is continuous, and we still have a role to play.

In Ephesians 2:10, that entrepreneurial tentmaker Paul says, as the New International Version translates it, "For we are God's handiwork, created in Christ Jesus to do good works, which God prepared in advance for us to do" (NIV).

That wasn't just true for Paul or Paul's audience in Ephesus. It's true for you and me, too.

We are God's handiwork.

We are called to do good works.

Today.

That was the real lesson I learned from reading the Bible. And I took it to heart. I booked a place in a Bible study course out in Australia and spent the next nine months in intensive study every day. By the time I made it back to America, I knew what I was meant to do—the purpose God had given me: to write *The Bible Study*.

If I was struggling as a lifelong devoted church-goer to understand God, the Bible, and my place in the world, surely other young Christians were feeling the same. Wouldn't it be useful to have a book that spoke to them in their language, in their context, so that they could make a little more sense of the whole Bible?

That seemed like a purpose worth pursuing.

God's story is ongoing, and that was the part I had to play in it. We're all here to fulfill a role in that story—we all have a similar purpose. Unfortunately, few of us have learned of that purpose through a whirlwind coming out of the desert or a vision on the road to Damascus. Today, God reveals our purpose to us with a bit more nuance.

But it is there within us.

All we have to do is discover it.

2

Purpose Comes from God

David is one of the most compelling people in the Bible—and for obvious reasons. There's the battle against Goliath and the journey to becoming king, the ups and downs of his fortune, and the scandals. It makes for great reading.

But I think what makes David so compelling thousands of years later is his origin. He was a nobody with no clear outward signs of greatness. He wasn't the son of a king or a great general or even a successful musician. He was simply the youngest son in his family tasked with the uninspiring work of watching the sheep.

All that came afterward occurred because he felt this intense purpose, a burning need to play his harp.

You can imagine him sitting up in the hills of Bethlehem strumming away day and night. There was no one to entertain. He couldn't make a single dollar off of his talent. But something compelled him to keep playing all the same. Something was driving him to play—something divine.

If David hadn't practiced his harp every day, he never could have become the boy with such amazing musical skill he used to ease the troubled mind of Saul.

WE ARE DESIGNED TO SEEK MEANING

When I was younger, I was very interested in hearing the wisdom of older, successful people. I chose to work in high-end hospitality for that very reason.

While I was saving up and scheming for a Big Idea that would allow me to become an entrepreneur, I took advantage of my circumstances to learn all I could from the people I met. I figured I could mimic their best habits to achieve a similar kind of success.

So any time I encountered an older, wealthy individual, I would ask the same question: "If you were twenty-two all over again, what would you do differently?"

The answers were always interesting, partly because they were always similar. No one said they wished they'd worked longer hours or invested more in stocks. The answers were always *deeper* than that.

I wish I'd spent more time with my kids.

I wish I'd been there for my family and friends more often.

I wish I'd left the desk job and pursued my dreams sooner.

I wish I'd gone into business on my own instead of climbing the corporate ladder.

In other words, what they all wished they'd done sooner, faster, and more often was focus on their purpose.

Whether that purpose was in their role as a parent, a spouse, a friend, or an entrepreneur, if they could roll back the clock, they would have put more of their hours into what gave their life meaning.

According to Victor Frankl, we are all born to pursue meaning and purpose in life. Frankl developed a theory called logotherapy during his time in the Nazi concentration camps. He was the only member of his family to survive the Holocaust, and what he noticed when observing his fellow survivors was that it was their purpose that kept them alive.

Those who felt some positive sense of purpose were more likely to make it through even the most horrific circumstances. Purpose—often creative purpose—unlocked something within them. It gave them life, even when others were trying to take it away.

DIVINE PURPOSE

We thrive through purpose because we were created *with purpose*. God did not make us haphazardly. According to Psalm 139, we are "fearfully and wonderfully made."

You know this already. It's why you're here. You have some nagging sense that you were made to be an entrepreneur. It draws your interest.

You feel passion for it.

You didn't choose this purpose. It's just something in you.

And you feel more like yourself any time you connect with it.

I'm the same way. I was designed to be an entrepreneur. I've known from childhood what God had made me for. I was born into a family that merged creativity and business. My mother transformed her trials against cancer into authorship. My father, meanwhile, was a movie producer for years and is also a legend in incentive sales up in Minnesota.

I took those influences and started my first business when I was nine years old. During an annual visit to Naples, Florida, I made necklaces out of shells and shark teeth. I walked up and down the beach, selling them for ten dollars a pop.

How's that for enterprising?

Ever since, there's hardly been a moment when I wasn't pursuing some potential business idea.

Before I graduated college, I'd written two books, owned a music booking agency, developed a clothing line, founded a social movement inspiring people to smile more, and recorded a lot of music. After graduation, I co-founded a recording studio, opened another clothing company, and crafted a pilot episode for a TV show concept.

There's no way to look at my life and see anything other than one purpose: entrepreneurship.

I'm sure you're the same way. Maybe you haven't actually founded a business yet—or maybe you've founded a dozen. Either way, that burning need to follow that path is in you.

And that need comes directly from God.

PURPOSE IS A FORM OF WORSHIP

It's impossible to look back at David's story and see anything but an act of divine purpose. And therefore, it's impossible to look at the author of the Psalms as anything but performing an act of worship in playing that music.

Maybe your purpose is to be a freelance musician like David. Or maybe it's to start a design agency or software company.

In whatever direction your entrepreneurial drive takes you, performing that work is an act of worship—so long as that work fits into God's plan.

David playing the harp was an act of worship because he made himself a vessel for God's plans. When Samuel came to him and sent him from the empty Bethlehem hills to the court of the king, he didn't flinch. He went where God called him.

It was in opening myself up to God's plan that I found my purpose as well. My previous entrepreneurial efforts had all been for me and my benefit. Once I placed God first, the path forward cleared.

The same is true for you.

Practicing the guitar is worship.

So is designing logos or writing code.

Same with making pasta.

Or grooming dogs.

...So long as you are performing those acts *for God.*

In pursuing our purpose, we must become good mimics. As Paul told the Ephesians in chapter five, verse one of his letter: "Therefore be imitators of God, as beloved children."

In the pursuit of entrepreneurship, that means you must imitate His purpose in yours. That requires your part in the story to come second behind His plan. You aren't playing guitar to get famous, and you aren't coding an app to get rich. You have to do this with God driving your motivations. You have to act in partnership with Him and always put His expectations before yours.

That's the key to success in a business that has meaning. That's how you find your purpose.

And once you know what you're looking for, you may find that purpose is closer than you could have ever imagined.

3

Finding Your Place in God's Story

There was once a Persian farmer named Ali Hafed. One night, a priest visited Ali. They spoke through dinner and late into the night, and eventually, their conversation turned to diamonds. The priest convinced Ali that he could do anything in the world—even buy a whole nation—with just a handful of the rare jewels.

That night, Ali couldn't sleep for all his thoughts of wealth. The next morning, he set off to make his fortune. He sold his farm, put a neighbor in charge of looking after his family, and gathered together all of his money to put toward his search for those precious stones.

He traveled the world—wandering through Uganda, Palestine, and Europe—but his efforts were fruitless. When he no longer had any money to his name, he ended up killing himself on the shores of Barcelona.

It's a very sad story...but it doesn't end there.

Some time after Ali's passing, the new owner of his farm took his horse out for a drink in the river that ran through the middle of the land. As the horse drank, a flash of light caught the farmer's eye. He reached into the river and pulled out a black stone that seemed to reflect all of the colors of the rainbow. It was so alluring, he took it, set it on his mantel, and went back to his work.

A few days later, that same priest walked into the house and saw the stone.

"Ali! Ali!" he shouted excitedly. "You've done it!"

"Ali has not returned," the farmer said. "This is now my land."

The priest was shocked. "But where did you find this enormous diamond?"

For a diamond it was. When the farmer and priest went out to the river and began to dig, they discovered one of the largest diamond deposits on the planet—right outside Ali's house.

GOD HAS GIVEN YOU EVERYTHING YOU NEED

My friend Ben Hoar heard that story at a conference in LA a few years back. Called "Acres of Diamonds," it was extremely famous in the early twentieth century. The most famous teller, Russell Conwell, delivered a speech on it over six thousand times.

The most amazing fact about it—the reason it has captured the minds of so many over the last century—is that it's absolutely true.

Incredible, right?

But what does it have to do with you?

So often, when we want to embark on a big enterprise, we think we need *something*.

We have to go somewhere.

We have to study some subject.

We have to meet some expert.

We have to be better than we are now in some fundamental way.

We assume something is missing, and that's why we don't have purpose.

I have suffered from these same assumptions. When my first efforts to get *The Bible Study* off the ground weren't immediately successful, I wondered whether I needed to go to seminary, become a pastor, build a reputation, *and then* reconsider what my purpose truly was.

But that thought was just a lack of confidence in myself—and in God's ability to bring the best out of me. I didn't need another degree or a bigger platform. God had placed everything I needed within me already to see and pursue my purpose. My experiences, skills, and passion were designed by God to show me the way forward.

I didn't need to wander the world for the direction I was lacking; the diamonds were right in front of me.

That's not to say you should stop learning—far from it—only that your purpose is already within you. Your faith, talents, knowledge, and experience have prepared you for your place in God's plan. You just need to understand what God is trying to tell you.

You have a role in God's story, and God has put all the qualities you need to play that role within you. Instead of seeking something outside of yourself, you should focus on clarifying what that role really is.

CLARIFYING YOUR PURPOSE

You know already that God has designed you for entrepreneurship. That's why you're here. The problem is you only have a vague sense of what you are meant to do as an entrepreneur. Even if you know that you want to open a barbecue restaurant or own an art supplies store—how do you make that business matter in the eyes of God?

And if God has placed the answer within you...where is it?

This can be particularly tricky since we often have false starts when finding purpose. I didn't know at twenty-two that my purpose would be to clarify the meaning of the Bible. I still thought I'd make it in the music business. And if not, there was always the clothing line.

As pastor and writer John Mark Comer once put it, "Sometimes a calling is staring us in the face. We just need to make eye contact."

In other words, finding purpose is often a matter of paying close attention—looking at ourselves in the mirror and looking for the purpose that is staring right back at us.

Listening to God's Voice

God tries to make purpose obvious for us, but for some reason, people just don't like to listen. The Bible is full of stories of people who outright refuse to hear what God is telling them. Adam and Eve didn't listen and ate from the Tree of Knowledge. That didn't work out so well for humanity, yet their son Cain went ahead and ignored God's word again—making an even bigger mistake.

Time and again, when God shows someone their purpose, they pretend they can't see it.

I was writing books from the beginning of college, but when I couldn't get the first couple published, I simply gave up and started looking for a different business opportunity. The inkling to create *The Bible Study* was always within me. I had simply turned my face away from it at the first sign of struggle.

Even Moses closed his eyes to God at first. When he encountered God in the wilderness in the form of a burning bush—a literal burning bush speaking with the voice of God—he really didn't want to hear what God had to say. This was God Himself coming to meet a lowly man in exile, sending as clear a message as possible about his purpose: "Bring my people out of Egypt."

You'd think if you received clear instructions like that you'd obey, right?

Not Moses.

He did everything he could to get out of it.

"Who am I that I should go to Pharaoh and bring the children of Israel out of Egypt?" he asked God.

Save my people? Bring them closer to You? Maybe You're thinking of a different Moses?

In total, Moses tried to get out of his purpose *five times* before God finally convinced him.

Despite the clearest sign imaginable, Moses nearly missed his purpose!

These days, God is rarely so explicit with us—but that doesn't mean He's calling us any less urgently. We may not be visited by burning bushes or walk with God in the Garden, but He constantly speaks to us and tells us the direction in which our purpose lies.

His word is just as valuable and just as easy to miss.

...Depending on which word that is.

In Greek, there are two words that mean "word"—the most basic component of conversation: *logos* and *rhema*. Both come up in the Septuagint—the Greek translation of the Old Testament Paul and other early followers of Jesus would have used—as equivalents of the Hebrew word *dabar*, or "Word of God."

Logos is the Greek used to describe Jesus at the beginning of the Gospel of John.

"In the beginning was the *logos*..."

Logos stands for the whole of God's revelation: His Son, His Book, His Spirit. These are the broad strokes of God revealing Himself to humanity. It's like He's using a bullhorn to address all of us with *logoi* that are timeless.

Logos is God's story written across time. It's perfect and unstoppable.

But that doesn't mean He's stopped pulling each of us aside for a quiet word. He still communicates to us individually through *rhema*.

Rhema implies something far more personal. This is more of a whisper from God that guides not humanity but each person individually.

The problem with *rhema* is that we can miss it. *Logos* never fails, but people from Adam on down have made a habit of missing *rhema*.

So how do we hear this *rhema*? And how do we make sure we follow it?

We have to spend a lot of time in prayer. This isn't prayer as a list of demands but prayer as an opportunity to listen.

Henri Nouwen, author and priest, said it well:

> *"The real work of prayer is to become silent and listen to the voice that says good things about me. To gently push aside and silence the many voices that questioned my goodness and to trust that I will hear the voice of blessing—that demands real effort."*

In other words, pray to hear God's *rhema*, and then listen closely as it lifts you up and directs you.

Outside of prayer, we might experience *rhema* as a gut feeling. I heard Julia Veach from Zoe Church refer to it as "knowing it in your knower."

Knowing it in your knower.

I like that.

You know how sometimes an idea seems to come out of nowhere and just feels right? It feels like it's supposed to happen? That's *rhema*. It can come up in a dream or a daydream. It can come from the wisdom of others. It shows up in a million ways, but we all know it when we see it.

We know it in our knower.

But what about all those ideas we just *know* are right but somehow don't work out—like my career as a designer?

That's another way God speaks to us. When our gut instincts line up with His wishes, things just start to come together. That person you could never get on the phone finally calls back to hear about your idea. An investor comes along eager to put some money behind your dream. Doors that were once bolted shut start to open up.

That's God's work in action.

God speaks to us in many different ways. The important thing is to be attentive to all the ways He communicates and to meet His words with obedience. We have to do better than Moses and try to meet God's expectations for us as soon as we encounter them. When He points us in a direction—even with the faintest of whispers—we need to follow.

Leaning into Your Talents

If all we had from God was *rhema,* most of us would never achieve our purpose. It's just so hard to know what is *rhema* from God and what is our individual preference. I pursued multiple careers *thinking* I was doing what I was meant to, but I was off course for years.

Luckily, God has given us more than a gut instinct for purpose. He's provided us with individual, unique strengths.

People are always saying we should work on our weaknesses, but I disagree. I think we need to double down on our strengths—because those strengths are heaven-sent.

"For you created my inmost being," David says of God in Psalm 139. "You knit me together in my mother's womb."

God was intentional in how He made us. We should run toward the strengths He put in us.

He created us on purpose, with purpose, and with the talents we need to fulfill that purpose. In fact, we can see this in David's story. When David is described to Saul in 1 Samuel 16, he is said to be "skillful in playing, a man of valor, a man of war, prudent in speech, and a man of good presence, and the LORD is with him."

Keep in mind, at this point, David is just a young shepherd. He hasn't defeated Goliath or even been in a battle yet. He's never played the harp for Saul.

Most of his conversation is with sheep.

Yet God has put all the qualities David will need to achieve his destiny in him already. God didn't speak to David in a burning bush like Moses, but David's purpose *is just as clear* because it's *so obvious* in his talents.

That's why you have strengths. God didn't create you to be good at everything, He created you to be incredibly good at a couple things—and to use those things you're good at to live your purpose and spread the Kingdom.

Focusing on your weaknesses moves you in the opposite direction from God's plans. The talent God didn't give you speaks as much to His plans as what He did.

For instance, I love music. When I was younger, I really wanted to be a rapper—I know, I know; don't judge.

I had the motivation. I just lacked one thing: the talent. I was terrible at it. I loved being in the studio and being around musicians, but when it came time to show what I had...I didn't have much. I would even forget my own lyrics onstage!

At one show, I actually wrote the lyrics on a piece of paper and read them off the page when I was supposed to be "feeling the music." Imagine the audience's reaction. Needless to say, my talents lay elsewhere.

But you know what? That's fine because music isn't my purpose. I still love it. I still like being part of that world, but it isn't what I was called to do. My talents led me in another direction.

Emphasizing Your Gifts

In addition to talents, God has provided all of us with spiritual gifts that allow us to positively impact the body of Christ in profound ways.

These gifts can come in a lot of different forms.

In the Bible, there are several lists of them, and while some gifts are clearly spiritual—prophecy, faith, miracles, tongues, interpreting tongues, healing, apostleship—many are not. Did you know that teaching is a spiritual gift? And leadership? And giving, mercy, wisdom, and administration?

Of course they are. *Everything we do in life is spiritual.*

The spiritual gift lists in the Bible are not meant to be exhaustive. Instead, they illustrate the ways that our gifts are meant to empower the Church and advance the common good.

Where do you see these types of gifts in yourself? Are you naturally a great explainer of complicated ideas to others? Does your faith often help people through their moments of doubt? Are you more adept at management and administration than anyone you know?

These gifts are meant to be used in God's plan by aligning us with God's wish that we love and take care of our neighbor. Paul actually makes this particularly clear by sandwiching his famous love chapter between his two lists of gifts. He's clearly telling us that God gave us gifts not to glorify us but to glorify Him by lifting each other up.

When clarifying your purpose, consider how you can channel your gifts into that purpose.

If you are a musician with a gift for teaching, perhaps part of your purpose is to teach music classes for the disadvantaged.

If you have a gift for administration, perhaps you help other bookstores with their inventory after you organize your own.

Or set up payroll to make sure every employee benefits as your business improves.

Trusting Your Experiences

As I mentioned before, I grew up in a household that seemed to be crafted in order to teach me all I would need to be an entrepreneur and writer. My father is a wise and successful businessman. My mother is an author. Faith was central to my youth as I witnessed God heal my mother four times from cancer.

When you look at it like that, how could I do anything but write *The Bible Study* and start my own business?

That's often the case with biographies. Steve Jobs's adoptive father was a machinist, and Jobs credited him for inspiring that love of machines that would allow him to change the world. Despite their future estrangement, Elon Musk's father clearly made an imprint on his son as an electromagnetic engineer who was also a sailor and a pilot.

No wonder Musk wants to engineer a way to reach the stars.

God often puts experiences in front of us to prepare our souls for the great tasks ahead. This isn't always a matter of a parent's profession. It could be friends you meet, setbacks you overcome, or a teacher whose message really spoke to you for a semester in high school.

We've all had these formative experiences. Imagine reading your own biography at the end of your life. What events would your future biographer pick out as showing the direction your life would turn?

Where would you see God moving in your life? What events would show He had opened a door?

Let these events act as markers in your life. Look for the direction they are pointing you and start moving that way.

Diving into Your Passions

What are you passionate about?

This may seem like an easy question for you. You know you're passionate about baking or design or law or writing. But that's not what I'm asking.

Your purpose is more than your interests, it's the passion you bring to creating a business *that matters*.

Let's say, after listening to God's *rhema* and looking at your talents, gifts, and experience, you realize you were made to own a coffee shop.

Your first memory is the smell of coffee. Over a cup of coffee, you're a natural conversationalist who makes everyone feel better. And you know how to roast the best beans in town. Great! That tells you the general direction your purpose will take you.

But what are you going to do to make that coffee shop *matter*?

That's where your passion comes in—not your passion for your talents or interests but for the things about the world that you want to see improved by God's love and justice.

What problems fire you up?

What change do you dream of seeing in your lifetime?

What cause is worth your time, energy, and dedication?

Maybe you're upset about global warming or the number of homeless we have in the country or human trafficking.

Maybe you're angry that there are children in the world with no shoes on their feet or people who work all day every day in the field and still can't earn enough to live on.

Maybe you wish we could save the bees or make sure everyone has clean water to drink.

That passion is crucial to truly fulfilling your purpose in God's eyes.

As much as your talent is from Him, so is this passion.

Working in partnership with God means putting His priorities to love our neighbor at the forefront.

If you care about global poverty, you should buy fair trade coffee beans exclusively for your coffee shop.

If you run a restaurant and care about homelessness, part of your purpose involves donating unused food to organizations that feed the hungry.

If it breaks your heart to see whales and sharks dying off at an alarming rate, live up to your purpose by donating some of your profits to cleaning up the oceans.

The businesses that really matter put these passions first—and that passion makes their success. Scott Harrison from Charity: Water was a nightclub promoter in New York. He had all of the "success" he could ever dream of, but he was on the brink of losing everything. That is until a trip to Africa opened his eyes to the urgency for clean water around the world. Only by merging this new passion with his previous experience was he able to build a new company *and* make it matter.

He has raised $370 million toward clean drinking water so far.

Let that be an inspiration.

With just a cursory glance, you can find meaningful companies everywhere. Patagonia donates 1 percent of sales to grassroots environmental causes. For every pair they sell, TOMS Shoes gives away a pair of shoes to a child somewhere in the world living without shoes.

These passions matter to God. After all, our God is a jealous God—one who cares deeply about His people. We can see that in how Jesus behaves in the Gospels.

There's a version of Jesus you see in our culture that depicts Him as extremely easygoing and relaxed. That's not the Gospel Jesus most of the time. Gospel Jesus was worked up about some social issues. He was passionate about caring for strangers and feeding the homeless and healing people. He was extremely upset about those who were meant to represent God to the people trying to make a profit off of Him. (You may remember an incident in the Temple.)

God gave us His Son's example because He wants us to be worked up about the problems in this world. He wants us to develop solutions to bring the Kingdom closer. And He wants us to work toward those solutions through our purpose.

CHURCH IN THE WILD

Tiago Magro is an artist friend of mine. He creates colorful graffiti-influenced gallery paintings and giant murals all around the world.

Tiago is originally from Brazil, and some of the passion behind his purpose is to bring his beautiful art and message of love to his country of origin.

A few years ago, he was having a conversation about this with a fellow Brazilian at Art Basel in Miami.

He mentioned that one of his big ambitions was to cover an abandoned church with his art. Suddenly, it felt like they were destined to meet and embark on this project together.

They began looking into it, and they ended up finding an abandoned church that was just sitting on a man's farm in Cuiaba, Brazil. They reached out and received permission to turn the church into an art exhibit.

To bring life and beauty to something that was forgotten.

When I heard about it, I told Tiago I was joining, even if that meant I just cleaned his paintbrushes the entire time.

We flew to Brazil with our friend Ray and shared the most incredible, inspiring experience—watching that abandoned church transform into a piece of art dedicated to God and love over a ten-day period.

On the last day, we had a church service in which communion was given by an evangelical pastor and a Catholic priest to show that everyone was welcome.

Before Tiago started painting, all of the locals said that the building was haunted. Now it is a point of pride for that community, and a place where anyone can come and worship Jesus.

That's what it means to make a business bigger than your interests or aptitude.

God crafted Tiago to make that church. He has been crafting you and leading you toward more than just entrepreneurship. You are a partner in bringing us closer to Him again.

But that doesn't mean that the path to success in business will be easy. Just as the Israelites had to come through forty years in the wilderness to find their promised land, there are many challenges ahead.

Knowing your purpose is only the beginning. Before you can turn that purpose into a Big Idea that changes the world and advances the Kingdom, you have to prepare for the trials to come so that you can be sure to fulfill God's destiny for you.

Part II

Preparing for the Wilderness

4

Removing
Obstacles

Abraham doubted God's plan. So did Moses. And Job. And Peter. These great movers of God's story all struggled, not from a lack of clarity about their purpose, but from mental hesitation. They saw the tough road ahead and simply couldn't believe God could provide a way through.

You can imagine Abraham trying to work it out in his mind.

> *I believe in God and my covenant with Him, but Sarah and I are getting old. Can God really deliver us a son?*

Or Peter:

> *I know Jesus is the Son of God, but surely He doesn't want me to put my life at risk for Him right now. Better to deny Him and get out of this situation.*

In my own journey with God, I've let mental blocks trip me up time and time again. I would toss the books I wrote in a drawer when I couldn't get any interest. I walked away from a clothing line because it didn't pick up traction fast enough—according to my expectations.

Each time I encountered a setback, I let it hold me back.

I wanted success quickly. I wanted it to come without struggle. And when it didn't come in my way, on my timeline, I would move on. I wasn't lazy; I simply let my mental obstacles block the way forward from what God had plotted for me.

I was lucky that God was patient enough to wait for me to figure this out.

MANY SETBACKS ARE MENTAL

Just because God is on your side and your goals are aligned with His doesn't mean it's a straight, smooth road to entrepreneurial success. Ask Moses how easy it was to deliver the Israelites from Egypt, even with all of God's creative and destructive powers focused on the effort.

The act of developing a Big Idea, opening a business around that idea, driving sales, and finding enough success to sustain yourself is going to be tough. In fact, finding purpose in business—as we saw in Part I—is often the *easiest* part of this journey.

I hope you're limbered up now. The way ahead is about to get really tough.

You'll face complex, labor-intensive, and time-consuming obstacles as you go forward in your entrepreneurial endeavor. We'll cover ways to resolve many of these in the chapters ahead. First though, I want to spend this chapter discussing your biggest obstacle: yourself.

For all the difficulties ahead, your biggest challenges will be internal:

Can you maintain belief and focus in your ideas, your business, and your partnership with God?

These internal struggles can appear suddenly or gradually at any point in this journey. Abraham doubted after he'd confidently agreed to a covenant with God. Peter's internal conflict was just before the crucifixion. Job's turmoil lasted an entire book of the Bible, while Moses needed reassurance upfront.

Your conflict can take on different characteristics, stemming from such diverse internal issues as time management, a struggle with accepting advice, and self-doubt. By tackling these mental obstacles first, you will be far better prepared for when they show up in the days ahead.

MANAGING TIME

"I wait for the Lord," says the psalmist in Psalm 130, "my soul waits."

Waiting is a natural part of Christianity. We await the Kingdom, after all. You would think, then, that we'd be good at waiting. But that's not the case. We may be content to wait for the Lord's return, but we want success now.

Most people are mental sprinters by nature. They gear themselves up for a quick burst of effort to reach a finish line a short distance away.

The problem for entrepreneurs is that building a business that matters is an ultra marathon.

The only way to fulfill your purpose and create a business that can survive every setback is to tackle time head-on by using it well upfront and refusing to set a deadline for success—you're in this for the long haul.

Maximize Your Time

I interviewed social entrepreneur and author Justin Zoradi for my senior thesis in college, and he introduced me to one of the greatest business lessons I've ever encountered: the law of compound interest.

In investment, compound interest is when the interest on your investment is based on the total amount you have invested instead of the initial amount. If you invested $500, a simple investment would give you interest on that $500. Compound interest, on the other hand, would increase as your investment grew. So as soon as that $500 became $600, you'd get interest on $600. The difference between simple and compound interest can be the difference between a mediocre investment and one that makes you rich.

But Zoradi's advice wasn't about investing money; it was about investing *time*.

If you build on small time investments in your business, you can achieve incredible things. Zoradi suggested that every single day you should do something—just a little something—that gets you closer to your dream. Imagine if you dedicated one hour a day to building your purpose into a business. That investment would pay off because every day you'd be building on what you did the day before.

You would be achieving compound interest on your purpose.

And instead of just working for an hour every Tuesday, you're now much further ahead because of the small investments compiling every day.

This is precisely how I wrote *The Bible Study*. Instead of wait-ing for inspiration to strike and then trying to write every-thing down all at once, I concentrated on writing a chapter a week. That required a page or so a day. Every day. Until it was done.

Some days the writing went well. Some days, not so well. But each day I made a little progress. And I had a rough draft of a full manuscript far sooner than I thought possible.

To plot out a compound interest plan, I recommended reverse engineering your goals—a.k.a. working backward. You start by making a list of all you need to accomplish to transform your purpose into a reality. If you want to be a furniture designer, you need to do research on your industry. You'll need to email people and build contacts. You'll need a business name. You'll need legal advice on copyrighting your designs. You'll need lots of sketches to begin the development process. You'll need some marketing know-how to get the word out about your stuff. The list goes on and on.

I know what you're thinking. *Who has time for all that?*

You're working a full-time job.

You have friends, family, a romantic partner, and a dog.

You have church and volunteering commitments.

You need to work out.

You need some time to relax.

And what about that new Netflix series?

Here's the thing: most of us have more time than we realize.

Unfortunately, we tend to learn this lesson only in retrospect. We look back on our youth and realize some crazy things. First, we looked great! Second, we had so much energy! And third, we had so much time!

If you haven't yet observed this in retrospect, I'll let you in on a secret: the only reason you feel like you don't have time is because you don't prioritize what you're spending it on.

If you really want to fulfill your purpose and create a business that matters, you have to choose to make that your priority. If you don't have an hour free each day, find a way to make that time. You don't have to hang out with friends every single night. You don't have to watch football every Sunday. You can skip that Netflix series everyone is talking about. You can stop reading everyone's posts on Instagram.

When I was getting started in entrepreneurship, I made a habit of sharing meals with friends, instead of seeing them at night.

I'd hang out for an hour or so over dinner with a friend to recharge—I had to eat anyway, why not in company? This one simple decision freed up my evenings to work on my projects.

It was a win-win solution for me and may not work for you, but you do have to make choices. If being an entrepreneur is part of God's design and purpose for you, you have to ask yourself: what are you willing to give up to achieve that purpose?

Once you see time not as an obstacle but as a resource you have to spend carefully, you'll start seeing opportunities in your schedule. And once you have that one hour free a day, you can do amazing things. All you have to do is choose one of the requirements above to open that design studio and start working away. It may be rocky at first; you may make mistakes, but the constant effort will pay off in the end.

Don't Expect Immediate Success

When you're constantly investing your time in your purpose every day, you may feel tempted to put a horizon on that effort. After all, it makes it so much easier to motivate yourself to get out of bed.

Just a couple more years, and I'll be successful. Then I can sleep in every morning at my new villa in Bali.

Trust me, you don't want to do that. Part of the crisis I had when my clothing line and music business failed was due to the deadline I'd given myself for success. When success didn't happen by the time I thought it should, I gave up, and my whole life fell apart.

You aren't on your timeline, you're on God's, and He can schedule things pretty far out into the future. Don't forget that He had His own chosen people wander for forty years in the desert before they reached the Promised Land.

Paul spent three years studying in Arabia before he took up his calling. That was *after* his vision on the road to Damascus.

David was anointed king fifteen years before he took his position of power.

God's own Son was in His thirties before He redeemed humanity. And that redemption took place thousands of years after the fall!

You can't guarantee He's going to make you rich by next Christmas. Or ever.

Of course, overnight successes do happen, but even in those cases, "overnight" is usually shorthand for years and years of preparation before sudden success.

LeBron James wasn't an overnight success. He practiced every day from childhood to become the greatest player of his generation in his teens. Or, as arguably the greatest soccer player in history, Lionel Messi, put it: "I start early and I stay late, day after day, year after year. It took me seventeen years and 114 days to become an overnight success."

Even those we consider obviously cut out for success struggled for years before achieving success or recognition.

Steven Spielberg was rejected from film school twice.

Stan Lee didn't publish a comic book until he was thirty-nine.

Samuel L. Jackson didn't make it big until he was forty-six.

Morgan Freeman was fifty!

Stephen King's first book was rejected thirty times by publishers. Dr. Seuss was rejected twenty-seven times.

They're now two of the most widely read authors in history, but there was nothing immediate about their success.

Clearly, even great talent doesn't ensure a quick rise. You have to be prepared to put in the work—every day—and to keep doing it for years to come. No deadlines. This is just life with purpose from here on out.

ADVICE FROM OTHERS

Advice may not seem like much of an obstacle, but in receiving, processing, and acting on advice, we face many internal obstacles. After all, we don't blindly follow every piece of advice we receive. We have to make choices, and those choices bring with them real consequences.

When I was going to print for the first edition of *The Bible Study*, I reached out to a few people I respected and asked for advice. One of those people was a fairly well-known evangelist, and his advice was simple: don't print a thousand copies. Don't assume you'll sell that many. Ever.

"Most likely," he told me, "you'll sell a hundred copies to friends and family, and then you'll be stuck with nine hundred books sitting around. Don't do that to yourself."

Start small, he said. Start slow. Wait and see if there's interest.

I didn't listen to him.

I printed that thousand copies, and I sold out of that first printing within three months. If I'd taken his advice to heart, I never would have been able to fill that first order and scale as quickly as I did.

Of course, sometimes advice is exactly what we need. Paul McCartney famously wanted to sing about scrambled eggs until John Lennon suggested maybe a more somber tone about a lost love from yesterday.

Choosing whose advice to listen to and when to listen to it is a tricky mental obstacle. The wrong advice can lead to bad decisions and a lack of self-belief. Good advice can save a whole business.

So how do you know the difference?

You start by considering who is giving it.

When you're undertaking a bold task—like creating a business that matters in partnership with God to advance His Kingdom—everyone has something to say. Some of them mean well; others may want to tear you down. And plenty will have opinions without knowing much of anything about your ideas or your journey.

Who are the people you trust in your life?

Who among your friends and family have experience in business worth learning from?

Do you have any mentors who know about the business world?

As we will see in the next chapter, these people should be a constant source of support, and they should be the ones you go to first for advice.

That doesn't mean you should refuse to hear anyone else out, but before you consider what they are saying, consider the source.

What are their motives?

Do they mean well?

Do they have the wisdom to offer good advice?

Only if they satisfy these questions should you mull over their words.

Once you know who to listen to, you have to decide how to take what they're saying. The evangelist who told me to limit my print run was a friend. He'd written books. He knew a lot about my subject and the world of book publishing. He was someone I should listen to by all means. So why didn't I follow his advice?

Unfortunately, this is a bit trickier than limiting your advisors. Wanting to give good advice doesn't mean the advice will be good. Well-meaning friends give bad advice all the time. How do you know the difference?

You trust your gut—your knower.

While others will try to assist you, this is *your* business and *your* purpose. You are the one in partnership with God in this task. So you have to make the final call. Remember that God often speaks to us through *rhema*—a whisper that can be as subtle as a gut feeling that a piece of advice is good or bad.

Of course, you can only trust *rhema* if you trust your instincts. If you don't have that internal trust, it's hard to steer through any internal obstacle. So in a way, self-doubt is the biggest obstacle you face.

SELF-DOUBT

For the longest time, I felt like an imposter. I was trying to write a book to help people understand the Bible, but I was no scholar. I didn't have a degree in theology. I wasn't a pastor. I had never run a million-dollar business. Who was I to write this book?

I felt like a fraud.

And I was in good company.

According to a recent article in the *Journal of General Internal Medicine,* as many as 82 percent of people experience imposter syndrome at some point in their lives. But this isn't a sign of failure; if anything, imposter syndrome is a sign you're heading down the right path.

When God is working for you, it can feel like you're rising faster than you should, taking on bigger challenges than you can handle, and succeeding beyond your abilities.

The Bible is filled with people suffering from imposter syndrome. Even Jesus asked God to pass the cup to someone else. My favorite self-doubter, though, is Jonah. Jonah was so certain he was the wrong guy for the job, he tried to flee to the other side of the world.

I have a tattoo of a whale on my forearm to commemorate the

act of God dragging Jonah back to his purpose, just like He did with me. That's how it is. We are far from being imposters; God is constantly trying to drag us in the direction He needs us to go.

So while it can feel like everyone else is smarter, more experienced, and more skilled than you, take comfort in realizing you're in good company. God's chosen people often feel that way. Maybe that's why He picks them.

To overcome this, you have to trust in God.

God wants you to be doing this. He designed you for this, and He's guiding you toward it.

That's why God didn't curse Moses for feeling like an imposter; He helped Him. While God was frustrated with the stubborn man denying Him in the desert, He didn't strike him down, He worked out a solution for his shortcomings.

Five times, Moses suggested there was something about him that wasn't good enough for this awesome task.

"Who am I to challenge Pharaoh?"

"What would I even say to these people?"

"What if they still don't believe me?"

"Don't you know I'm a terrible public speaker?"

"Isn't there someone else who's better suited for this job?"

Each time Moses protested, God had an answer: "I am with you. You can do this." Even as He lost patience, He stuck to the same message.

"I am with you. You can do this."

YOU AREN'T DOING THIS ALONE

God didn't just give Moses a divine pep talk, He offered a real solution. Moses wasn't a good public speaker—but his brother Aaron was. God suggested they work together to achieve His aims.

Just because you are in partnership with God in this doesn't mean you won't need others to help you along the way.

When you begin to face the reality of your pursuit of purpose in business, the first conclusion you might reach is that you aren't the right person for the task.

Someone else could do it better.

Someone else has more time for it.

Someone else wouldn't face all that criticism.

Someone else has all the right experience, skills, and connections.

In such moments, remember that you aren't doing this alone. God is with you. And as we'll see, God will provide you with others who can help you overcome whatever is ahead.

5

Better Together

Even though I turned out to be a terrible rapper and an unsuccessful record producer, I made a lot of my friends in the industry, and while I lived in Minneapolis, I would host them whenever they came to town. I'd show them around, take them out to cool restaurants, and enjoy being a small part of that awesome creative force for an evening or two.

One such weekend completely changed my life.

My friends, DJ Ray Rock and photographer Mike Folabi, were in town on tour. I picked them up from behind the venue, and we went to grab a bite to eat. We ventured to a little food stand in the back of Hmongtown Marketplace in St. Paul to have these incredible egg-roll-stuffed chicken wings and green papaya salad.

I live for experiences like that.

During our meal, Ray brought up Miami, where he lived.

"You've got to come down there," he insisted. "Visit once, and you'll never want to leave."

I was definitely intrigued. I had plenty of friends in Miami, and it seemed like my sort of city—full of art, great food, amazing culture, and far less snow—but I wasn't convinced.

The conversation went for a wander before Ray tried a different tactic.

"Are you seeing anybody?" he asked.

"No, not at the moment."

"You should check out this girl," he said, handing me his phone. The picture he had on the screen was of the most beautiful girl I'd ever seen.

"She lives in Miami?" I asked.

Ray nodded.

"Maybe I'll come down for a visit," I said, with a smirk on my face.

A month later, I was flying down to Miami for the first time. I got an Uber from the airport and drove to the house of my friend who was going to show me around for the weekend.

The first night we were going to attend a Friendsgiving with a bunch of people I had never met before. But when we arrived at the house, I knocked on the door, and guess who opened it?

The most beautiful girl I had ever seen. The girl from the picture—Gisela.

We spent the whole night together—talking, laughing, dancing. Just having a great time. When I got back to Minneapolis a few days later, we continued talking. And talking. For weeks.

And then in December...I hit a brick wall.

It turned out, she wasn't into me in *that* way. I was crushed, but I'm a determined guy—and I was convinced there was something *there*. So right after Christmas, I jumped on another flight down to Miami. Moments before I took off, I sent Gisela a text: "I'm flying down to Miami for the weekend. I have no plans except to see you."

It was the big, grand romantic gesture of my life.

And let me tell you, grand romantic gestures do not always work out. Particularly when you only let the other person in on it via text at 6:30 in the morning.

I should have known the day was doomed from the start. When I landed and checked my phone, I found out Gisela had some commitments in the morning and couldn't get to the airport for another hour and a half.

No problem, I thought, only half-convinced myself, *this is still a good idea.*

When we finally met up, I took her out for a romantic day that included a surprise sunset sailboat cruise. I had it all planned out. I just knew it was going to reconnect us and bring us back to those happy first few weeks of texting back and forth.

It was a disaster.

That connection we'd had on that first surprise meeting had completely evaporated. The whole thing was forced and super awkward. After we got off the boat, she said, "Are you going to be good here? I have to go play volleyball with my friends."

No invitation. No suggestion we meet up the next day.

"Sure," I said. "I've got some friends I'd like to see anyway."

"Great," she said, trying to be kind as she let me down. "Thanks for coming down."

The next month or so, we didn't talk. At all. When we did reconnect, there was more awkwardness. Finally, after six months of pursuing the woman of my dreams, I gave up.

And *that's* when she became interested.

I don't know what it was. As soon as I stopped trying so hard, all that original chemistry came back. The conversations were fun again. We kept getting closer.

We met up again in Miami, and then truly reconnected at Transformation Conference in Tulsa a couple months later. From that moment on, it all started to click into place.

I moved to Miami in October 2019.

In February 2020, I proposed.

In April 2020, we got married.

It's a happy ending, but our courtship was extremely up and down. One moment it was meant to be, the next it was over forever. A door would open on its own until I slammed it shut without knowing what I did wrong—until she came along and opened it again.

That's how love is. That's also how business is.

You have breakthroughs and then setbacks. It's clear sailing up until you hit an unseen patch of choppy water.

One moment you think you're onto something; the next, you think you have the worst ideas ever.

The next moment after that, you're going to be a millionaire.

A moment further on and you think you're going to have to file for bankruptcy.

To maintain focus and belief through it all, you need part-ners—people who understand you, believe in you, and help you through those rough moments on the way to success.

GOD CREATED US FOR HUMAN PARTNERSHIP

In Genesis 2:7, God breathes the "breath of life" into Adam. Except that isn't an accurate translation of the Hebrew. It isn't one life God breathes into Adam.

The Hebrew word for life—*chayim*—is plural. God, essentially, breathes *lives* into Adam. Which makes sense, because Adam's partner, Eve, was pulled *out of him*.

Two lives from one source.

The first human partnership comes about with the first two people, and it's born out of the fact that two lives were created, entwined as one. We see this same kind of intense partnership throughout the Bible: Abraham and Sarah; Jacob and Rachel; Boaz and Ruth.

But Biblical partnership goes well beyond romantic relation-ships. Moses and Aaron were partners, as were David and Jonathan. Jesus had the Twelve, and Paul had all of his helpers.

God has designed us for human, as well as divine, partnership. We are meant to be part of a community.

We are, after all, *the people of God*—a *society* of believers. God has made us this way because, when we are together, we strengthen one another. And when one of us takes on a monumental task, we need the strength and faith of others to achieve it.

Whatever part they play, partners are essential to our success. Think of David's life after Jonathan's death. Would Jonathan have ever allowed him to send Uriah to war for Bathsheba? Without a partner to help him, though, David gave in to his worst instincts.

This same dynamic is clear in modern business.

Steve Jobs was only able to rise as high as he did because he began his career with Steve Wozniak as a partner. Jobs was the dreamer, but Wozniak was the technician who allowed Jobs to show the value of his vision.

Likewise, Bill Gates didn't make Microsoft a success alone; he had Paul Allen by his side.

Ben's ice cream is only great because he has Jerry.

Bill Hewlett could only make a successful computer company with Dave Packard.

Even those entrepreneurs without a public partner have partnership in their life. When Jeff Bezos and MacKenzie Scott divorced, she received $38 billion from the settlement—in large part because she played such a valuable role in Bezos' development of Amazon.

These days, at The Brand Sunday, I'm lucky enough to have my own partner—one I intend to *stay* married to—in the form of Gisela and my own Wozniak in our Chief Operations Officer, Caleb Brose. I run every idea past Gisela. And Caleb's mastery of day-to-day operations has freed me up to focus on the creative side of the work.

I literally couldn't run the business without either of them.

That's how it always is. While the role a partner—or partners—plays is different for each entrepreneur, no one ever achieves success on their own. It always takes partners.

WHO MAKES A GOOD PARTNER?

Human partnership can involve a business partner or a romantic partner. It might also include a sibling or a mentor. They may have an active role in your business—or not. No matter their role, though, their purpose is to be someone to whom you remain accountable. No matter how much or how little success you see, there should always be someone there to remind you who you are, where you want to go, and how effectively you are getting there.

You need people who give you stability, people you can test out your ideas on and who will share their wisdom with you. You need people who believe in you and want to help you share your vision with the world. You need people who will pray for you and with you, listen to the Holy Spirit on your behalf, and put your dreams first.

You need people like Matt Richmann. He was perhaps my first partner in developing *The Bible Study*. He believed in me from the beginning and encouraged me when I lost faith in myself. He even helped me financially to get the book off the ground. We lost him last year to colon cancer, and the pain of losing a friend and a partner was immense. I am only here because of Matt's belief.

That's the kind of partnership you need when you're trying to achieve something in business that *matters*.

Who do you know who fits that bill?

Like Matt, a good partner shares your belief in your project and is passionate about changing the world. They are wise and pray for you. They are guided by the Holy Spirit and love and care about you and your well-being.

Ideally, they are smart and energetic and have experience, faith, and knowledge that will help you on the journey ahead.

Does this describe someone in your life? Great! Does it describe several people? Even better! Each partner may offer different qualities you need to draw from for different needs.

However, that doesn't mean your partners should become an expansive group. Partners should be particularly close to you and deeply knowledgeable of you and your life.

Think of how Jesus related to the apostles. He had twelve partners in all, but he was truly close to only two: John and Peter.

CHECK YOUR CIRCLE AND REACH OUT

When I was younger, I had tons of friends. As I've gotten older, though, I've come to realize that friendship is valuable not for its quantity but its quality. You don't have to have three hundred friends. There's no way to get close to that many people. Instead, you should put value in a few true friends who know you and love you best.

As I invested my free time in building businesses while also working full-time, I saw many friends drift away. They weren't interested in making the compromises required to maintain friendship with me. When I wouldn't blow off my responsibilities to hang out, they eventually stopped calling.

They weren't bad friends, but they were a bad fit for me because they didn't understand what I was trying to do or where I needed to get to. Obviously, they would have made bad partners.

So where do you find good partners?

Maybe you already have them.

You just have to "check your circle" first.

That's the phrase my pastor, Rich Wilkerson Jr. uses at VOUS Church. To check your circle, just look at your circle of friends and consider who among them is supporting you, helping you grow, and enabling you to become the person you're intended to be. Essentially, who will do whatever it takes to help you achieve your purpose?

It's okay to distance yourself from those who don't pass the check.

Letting people go from your life can be hard to accept in our social-media-driven world. But it's okay—even necessary—to let some friends drift away. You don't have to respond to every text or DM or make time for every person who wants to enjoy an evening out with you. If they understand you and believe in what you're doing, they'll work with you to accommodate that in your friendship.

I've been checking my circle for the last few years, and the result is a small group of friends that is extremely tight-knit and supportive of one another. I still have tons of acquaintances and casual friends that I enjoy seeing every now and again, but I concentrate on building those close relationships that I know will feed my needs as a person and an entrepreneur.

Of course, not everyone has a big circle to pull from when choosing partners. There were times when I needed a type of support my circle couldn't provide.

When I was eighteen years old, there was a six-month period where I would call Pharrell Williams's studio in Miami at lunchtime every single day to try to get advice from him. I was a huge fan of his entire approach to life, and his entrepreneurial mind inspired me.

But every day, the receptionist would put me on hold, and he never picked up. Looking back, I think it was a sign I needed someone to fill that mentor role in my life, and not to just connect with a celebrity.

To find that mentor, I had to go looking and take some chances. Perhaps you, too, need to seek out partners. Your friends may not really understand what you are about as a Christian, an individual, or a budding entrepreneur. It's critical, in that case, to seek out a community that will encourage and strengthen you as you move forward.

TATTOO IT ON YOUR HEART

Since Gisela and I have been together, I've realized the thing I needed most through those stressful, wonderful, mysterious months I was courting her was *her*—someone who understood me, who could comfort and advise me on the most intimate level. Someone who could have helped me plan my grand romantic gesture a little better.

That's exactly the role she fills at The Brand Sunday now. I run every decision past her. Anytime I need wisdom, I go to her first, because she is my counsel. She always knows the right answer. It's no exaggeration to say she's one of the main reasons we've grown to the level that we have over the last year.

Her wisdom, understanding, passion, and perspective combined with Caleb's organization, Matt's early belief, my parents' guidance and example, and the help of a dozen or more others along the way have all been crucial in building The Brand Sunday.

When you are ready to move beyond the concept of a business and into the reality of business, you're going to need that kind of support as well.

In my twenties, I tried to do everything on my own. I was going to be a business success without the help of friends, family, romantic partners, or even God. I wanted to fly solo.

And I couldn't do it.

The best decision I ever made was to allow others in, to choose to be in partnership with God, and to find partners among friends—and with Gisela.

There were so many difficulties ahead, so many obstacles I couldn't see from where I was in that moment, but I was able to overcome them all because I had the right people by my side. Once you have those people too, you'll be ready to take those first steps into the wilderness of building that God-given purpose you have discovered and turning it into a business that matters.

And that all starts with finding the Big Idea you can build that business around.

Part III

Creating Your Big Idea

6

Confronting Reality

It's easy to be fearless if you don't ever try anything. What's there to be scared of about a roller-coaster if you never intend to ride one?

Fear is all about the confrontation with something real. Like when I went snowboarding in Whitefish, Montana, for the first time. That should have been no big deal, really. You see, I grew up snowboarding in Minnesota.

But the mountains in Montana are on another level.

My friends, Brennen and Jason, and I took the train out west and figured we were in for the time of our lives.

Now, I've never been afraid of heights—but until then I'd never really been in a position where heights made much of a differ-ence in my life. As soon as that chairlift took off and I felt nothing but a hundred feet of air under my boots, I learned that I was actually terrified of heights! My legs were shaking. My stomach started turning. I put a stranglehold on the chairlift all the way to the top of the mountain.

Needless to say, I didn't enjoy the chairlift much.

Something similar happened when I was in Australia. I love the ocean. Seahorses are one of my favorite creatures on this planet of ours. And sharks? Like everyone else, I never skip the shark tank at the Seaquarium.

Sharks behind thick glass and sharks under the surface of the water you're swimming in are two very different things, though.

When I heard that the freshwater river we lived on flowed into the ocean, that there was a rope swing upstream, and that sometimes you could even see dolphins jumping out of the water, I thought, *awesome!*

...Except this river was a favorite little spot for sharks to gather for a quick meal as well. And while everyone said it was nothing to worry about, I couldn't shake it. Suddenly, I was terrified of sharks. Every time I jumped off that rope swing and landed in the water, I would flail around, trying to keep the sharks away. I'm sure it looked ridiculous, but just the thought that real sharks were swimming underneath my very real and delicious feet was too much for me. Even if it was all in my imagination. Because truthfully, there was no evidence that they were under me in the first place.

That's the nature of fear. It comes out when the idea of some-thing becomes a reality, when it stops being hypothetical or fictional and stares you right back in the eye.

NOW IT'S REAL

Almost everything you have done in the first two parts of this book is conceptual. Learning more about your faith and your place in God's story, searching for your purpose, preparing mentally for upcoming obstacles, and choosing your circle of partners are all extremely valuable, but you could achieve all of it without ever telling a single person your plans to create a business that matters—let alone taking steps to open an actual business.

At this point, though, all of the work begins to become exter-nal—and a lot more real. Once you've found your place in God's story and done the mental and social preparation, you have to start taking clear steps toward a very public purpose in entrepreneurship, and you can't hide where you are heading anymore.

This is the moment when you are going to find the ideas to propel your purpose forward and introduce them to the world.

It's a thrilling moment! It's also *absolutely* terrifying!

I've written several books, and I can tell you, it isn't scary to sit down and type out the words. The scary part is handing the manuscript off to someone else to read. Suddenly, you're exposed. There's no hiding or denying anymore—this is your heart and soul, the product of your greatest efforts, and if someone doesn't like it or it somehow doesn't work...

In other words, you have to admit to yourself and to the world that you are taking on a huge challenge. And that means you are now running the risk of a clear, undeniable, and public failure.

FACING UP TO FAILURE

"Failure" is such a brutal word in English. To call someone a failure is to dismiss everything they've done.

Whatever effort they've put in...

Whatever ideas they've come up with...

Whatever achievements they've attained...

It doesn't matter—none of it was good enough to succeed.

It's no wonder, then, that we have such a natural, sometimes overwhelming fear of failure.

The way to get over that fear, though, is to take the sting out of the concept. Everyone fails. In fact, failure is a key part of growth. Steve Jobs was fired from Apple. It was a huge scandal. Every newspaper in the world reported on it. A decade later, he came back to the company and invented the iPhone. Michael Jordan was cut from his high school basketball team.

If you've watched *The Last Dance,* you know how well he took that. He came back from it to become the greatest player of all time.

History is filled with these stories.

Thomas Edison's teachers thought he was too stupid to learn anything.

James Dyson, the inventor of the bagless vacuum, failed an astounding 5,126 times!

In the end, it isn't failure that keeps people down, it is the mindset you develop coming out of failure. As G.K. Chesterton put it: "How you think when you lose determines how long it will be until you win."

Walt Disney said of the early criticism he received, "It is good to have a failure while you're young because it teaches you so much."

So instead of trying to avoid failure, expect it and hope to learn from it.

Because failure is a necessary component of success. Every great book you've ever read was the product of a hundred failed drafts you never saw.

As former high school basketball failure Michael Jordan once said, "I've missed more than nine thousand shots in my career.

I've lost almost three hundred games. Twenty-six times I've been trusted to take the game-winning shot and missed. I've failed over and over and over again in my life."

What I'm saying is, if you fail, you are in great company. So what is there to fear?

DO NOT FEAR

You're still freaked out. I get it. Knowing that Michael Jordan missed the cut in sophomore year doesn't make the fear go away.

So maybe God can help. One of God's favorite phrases is "do not fear." He says it in the Bible more than 365 times—more than enough to fill an entire calendar. The meaning behind this is clear enough:

God is on your side every single day.

But this is not the only way God reassures us in the face of failure; He also shows us in almost every page of the Bible how He wants us to handle failure.

Humans are constantly failing in the Bible. They're falling short in their faith; they're running from responsibility; they're afraid to live up to their purpose. Adam failed to heed God's first commandment. Abraham, the man whose line leads us directly to God's own Son, was a constant failure. He didn't listen to God. He doubted. He broke the rules. When God promised him a son with Sarah, he got impatient and took advantage of his servant. When he went to Egypt, he became frightened and lied about his relationship with Sarah. The list goes on.

The Israelites failed to follow God's commandments in the desert.

The Kingdom of Judah regularly failed to heed the words of the prophets.

The Apostles failed to protect Jesus from arrest.

The only reason we have Paul's letters is because of his failures. Paul's efforts to establish churches across the Gentile world constantly faced setbacks. Letters were how he tried to fix those failures. In total, Paul wrote to Corinth at least four times—only two of his letters survived...that's a long story— because he and the church were constantly failing to understand each other and one another.

Through all of these failures, God has persisted in His plans. He has constantly and consistently tried to draw us back to Him.

But He has always required that we rise from our failures and try to reach out for Him again.

When you set out on this path, you are inviting failure. It's inevitable. Whether you fail big or small, failure will happen. The question, once again then, isn't how to avoid failure, but what to do with it.

WHAT TO DO WITH FAILURE

Failure is inevitable, so you have to learn how to live with it.

To limit the fear of failure when pursuing your purpose in business, you can start by keeping your day job. This, of course, requires more commitment from you—you have to find extra hours in the day to focus on *your* business—but it also lowers the stakes. If your first business effort fails, you aren't losing your income. You can still pay the rent. If you have a setback and have to delay launching, you can afford to wait.

As I mentioned before, I kept my day job *for years*, even after *The Bible Study* had become a success. It was only when we were making enough that I could afford to pay myself a full salary *and* invest heavily in the company that I jumped into it full-time.

Treating your business as a passion more than a career at first doesn't mean you can't succeed.

TOMS Shoes started out as a side project.

Steve Jobs still worked for Atari as he and Steve Wozniak built the Apple I.

Businesses from Instagram to Yankee Candle and Under Armor were all side projects in the beginning.

With that safety net in place, you can feel more comfortable taking a greater risk.

But that only softens the blow of failure. To truly come to terms with it, you need positive steps you can take to come out of failure stronger than before. For this, I find three perspectives particularly helpful.

First, look at failure as a way to develop the wisdom you need for success. As John Mark Comer said in his book *Garden City*, "If you fail at doing something you're not supposed to do, it's a success. Because with each success and with each so-called failure, you're getting a clearer sense of your calling."

This was certainly the case for me. I failed as a clothing designer because that wasn't my primary calling. And I certainly wasn't meant to be a rapper. Even though those failures were painful, they were good for me.

Second, jump right back in. When Stephen King faced a massive number of rejections and intense criticism early in his career, he got over it by simply continuing to work. He wrote through the pain of failure.

Finally, take a longer view of your life than just that moment of failure. Think of yourself as a ninety-year-old looking back. Ask yourself what would be worse: failing now or letting fear keep you from ever trying?

In my opinion, it's the latter. It's better to have loved and lost, and it's better to have tried and failed. Better still, to try, fail, and try again.

THAT FIRST BRAVE STEP

Failure seizes people right at the moment they're about to take their first step toward purpose. It's often that moment when they have to refine a sense of God's plan into an actual plan for their business that they begin to lose heart.

It's too complicated.

It's too hard.

I don't get how this works.

I'm just not ready.

I get it. Creating a business around a great idea *is* hard—but it isn't as hard as you think. In the chapters ahead, I'm going to give you an overview of the process to get you from a general sense of purpose to a business built on a Big Idea that speaks to an ideal customer.

Having these touchpoints won't keep you from ever failing, but they will keep you from stumbling out of the gate.

And that basic knowledge—combined with God's partnership and some bravery in the face of your fears—may just be enough.

7

What's the Big Idea?

***The Bible Study* came to me directly from God.** That's the only explanation for it.

In my parents' basement, after I had moved home from Australia and had all of this content ready to be shared, I closed my eyes in prayer and saw exactly what I was supposed to do. I saw my Big Idea—the idea that I could build my purpose around: a book that made the Bible accessible and less overwhelming to young Christians. I mean, I could *see* the book as clearly as if it were already in my hand.

I was blessed, to say the least. That's not usually how businesses—even businesses partnering with God—develop. God doesn't tend to get into the details with most people. A lot of the time He's more a "go to Nineveh and you'll figure out what to say when we get there" kind of God.

There's far more *rhema* in the plans He reveals than *logos*.

For some reason far beyond my comprehension, I was an exception. But even in my case, receiving my Big Idea didn't make the road ahead particularly clear.

How was I going to publish this book?

How could I make sure to attract new readers?

What images did I need?

How big was it going to be?

What additional materials would I need to create?

Oh, and by the way, what was I actually writing on the page?

To answer those questions, I had to do a ton of ideating—the process of coming up with a mountain of new ideas so you can pick the best ones.

That's how it always is in business. Whether God is spelling out your Big Idea or giving no more than subtle hints, it takes a lot of ideas to go from inspiration to execution. And it's those ideas that get you from a sense of purpose to living it.

MOVING BEYOND PURPOSE

In the first part of this book, we looked into what your purpose is in God's story. How do your talents, gifts, experiences, passions, and, above all, God's wishes come together to define your purpose?

But knowing you should be a baker is different than knowing what type of business to build around your baking skills. Are you going to open a bakery or sell baked goods to local restaurants and shops? Or do you want to design custom wedding cakes from your kitchen? Or sell online only?

Most importantly, how is that baking business—whatever it ends up looking like—going to stand out from all the other bakeries in the world?

That's what your Big Idea has to answer—not just a general purpose but a definitive business idea that can survive and thrive in the modern, hypercompetitive business world.

Big Ideas are not always easy to come by. They may take time and a lot of effort. They may come in pieces or all at once so quickly you'll miss it if you blink. To find one requires constant ideation that chips away at all the possibilities until you arrive at that one idea that speaks to you.

When Michelangelo carved the statue of David, people were obviously blown away by it. But some enterprising individual actually asked the great artist how he could sculpt something so beautiful out of a rock. It didn't even make sense to him.

Michelangelo responded that it was easy. "I chipped away the pieces that weren't David."

When searching for a Big Idea, we're all sculptors. Underneath that huge block of possibilities for all the potential bakeries in the world is the one bakery that is *your* bakery. Your task now is to cut away all the options that are *not your bakery* until you see your Big Idea clearly.

Even with crystal clear instruction to write *The Bible Study*, I didn't just sit down one day and type the book out. It was months and months of chipping away at that stone, finding the right book—*my book*—underneath.

It required a thousand different approaches. I wrote out chapters that had to be rewritten. I put down tasks I would later drop entirely. There were false starts and bad ideas throughout.

But eventually, after discarding 999 of my thousand approaches, I could see the shape of my Big Idea through all the rubble. And once I could make that out, it became easier to make my next cut.

THE SPLATTER APPROACH

Picasso once said, "Everything you can imagine is real," and nowhere is that more true than business. You are only limited by your imagination here. After all, someone came up with the idea of making a playground part of a burger joint. Someone else came up with the idea of designing jewelry for dogs.

They've made millions off those ideas.

The best way to channel your imagination into finding that Big Idea is an ideation technique that I like to call the Splatter Approach. The process is more Pollack than Picasso, but it's beautiful in its simplicity:

Throw absolutely everything at the wall and see what sticks.

At this point, there are no bad ideas.

Dream big.

Dream ridiculously big.

Dream small.

Dream sensible.

Even with the ideas that don't seem relevant. Put them all out there. Write them all down.

For instance, my biggest, boldest, most unbelievable dream right now is to eventually give away a billion dollars during my lifetime, all in the effort to finance young Christian entrepreneurs and the Church on a radical new level.

I won't be doing that next year. But it's a good idea! It's a Big Idea—even if it isn't the right idea for this particular moment.

The same way I developed that idea, I also came up with other projects at The Brand Sunday, like *The Best Season Planner* and *The Bible Study: Youth Edition* and the Christian wellness company Whole-y. It's the same way I came up with this book. I've also come up with a lot of terrible ideas, but those have gracefully been thrown out with the trash.

If you'd looked at my notebooks during the writing of *The Bible Study*, you would have thought I was incredibly unrealistic. Easily digested content for every book in the Bible? Quite a lot of work for a guy who doesn't have a theology degree. I only got where I am because I took that vision and put every big, foolish idea down in writing.

IDEATION PROMPTS

Whether you have a sense of your Big Idea and simply need to refine it or you only have the vaguest sense of purpose at this point, the Splatter Approach will be valuable in generating potential ideas for you.

However, coming up with potential Big Ideas isn't particularly easy. Even if you're ready to write down every thought, how do you get the ideas flowing? Where do you even start?

Perhaps with some questions to shift your mind into "world-changing business that matters" gear.

Sometimes, all it takes to find a brilliant idea is the right basic question. With that in mind, here are a few to get you thinking.

What would I create if money was no problem?

I hear it all the time:

>*"I'd start a clothing line, but it's too expensive."*

>*"I'd open a gym, but I don't have the investment money."*

>*"I'd run a doggie daycare, but who is going to finance that?"*

So often, the problem isn't a lack of a Big Idea; it's hesitancy to accept it. The Big Idea is right in front of you, but you convince yourself you can't pull it off.

This really gets back to that fear of failure we all struggle with. It seems fun to imagine climbing Everest, but when it comes time to pack your bags and fly to Nepal—it suddenly feels way out of your capabilities.

Me? Climb that thing? No way.

The thing is, "too expensive" or "too hard" isn't a reason to give up—certainly not on your purpose. It's an obstacle, undoubtedly, but not one you can't overcome with a good idea.

But the only way to find those ideas is to stop limiting yourself before you even try.

After all, how often do we hear about new tech products that required millions of dollars before they could make a cent? Somehow, they make it happen. Look at Tesla, an incredibly expensive Big Idea dream that took years to make a profit. It's now the world's most valuable car company. Who's to say your idea won't be next?

Besides, oftentimes, as we'll learn later, you can build a company on far less money than you assume. You can start a clothing line for less than you have in your bank account. Does that seem like it's unattainable?

Whether you need to find investors, find more affordable strategies, or make a few personal sacrifices, you can make your Big Idea a reality—so long as you allow yourself to dream it up. Once you have the idea, you can find the path to accomplish it.

So start by allowing yourself to dream. No idea, no matter how big or ridiculous, should be dismissed out of hand. After all, there was a time when rented office space seemed absurd, and when shopping online was ridiculous, and when commercial air travel seemed unworkable, and when indoor plumbing seemed a luxury that would never make it beyond wealthy homes.

Those things could only become realities because their inventors chose to dream first and figured out the *how* later.

What idea has been on my mind forever?

Your Big Idea may also just be something that's already occurred to you—an idea that keeps nagging away at you that you constantly dismiss. Do you love Cuban restaurants but know you have better recipes? Do you chat over the meal about how you want to run a food truck one day?

A Cuban food truck?

That's your idea.

Does it drive you crazy how big chain coffee shops don't give you a consistently good cup of coffee? Are you the person your friends come to if they want to learn about new pour over techniques or small batch coffee brands?

Bingo.

For me, writing a book about the Bible always made sense. My mother is a writer, and I'd already written two books. Writing has always attracted me. It was always within me. A book about the Book had been in the back of my mind for years before God showed me what that book would actually look like.

So what is it about your purpose that excites you? When your purpose comes up in conversation, where do your thoughts gravitate? Is there some particular part of your purpose that you always come back to over and over again?

Maybe there's a reason for that.

What problem can I solve?

Passion, belief, and direction won't amount to much if your Big Idea doesn't solve a problem for your future customers or make their lives easier and better in some way.

This is true of every successful product out there. Airbnb made it easier and cheaper for people to get accommodation on vacation. The hotels and resorts were too expensive and often didn't provide people with the space or location they were looking for. No wonder the company took off.

Likewise, Uber and Lyft solved problems people had with taxis: they were too expensive, lacked personality, and were never where you needed them to be.

Netflix made it possible for people to watch TV shows and movies whenever they wanted without having to visit a Blockbuster (remember those?) or pay a hundred bucks a month for cable.

And if you're old enough to remember the Walkman days—when you could only take one CD with you, had to constantly buy batteries, and were worried about tracks skipping—the iPod was a major upgrade across the board.

You don't necessarily have to be as revolutionary as these huge business successes, but you do need to provide people with something they don't already have. Maybe it's Cuban food in your food truck right downtown instead of a restaurant out in the suburbs. Or maybe it's designing shirts made out of recycled plastic. For me, it was making the Bible less overwhelming to younger people by speaking directly to them without speaking down to them.

In the end, it doesn't matter which problem you solve, you just have to solve one—otherwise people won't put the effort into getting your product.

How do I incorporate God into this idea?

Finally, before you move forward with your new Big Idea, you need to pull back and get some perspective by asking:

How am I going to bring God along here?

If you've been following along, this is something you've already given some thought to, but you have to regularly check back in on this priority—your top priority—as you go along. Having a general sense of direction in God's story is different than having a clear idea you are pursuing as a business with God in partnership.

While the questions above are the most important from a business perspective, this is really the most important for you as a Christian. After all, this isn't just another business you're creating. This is a business that means something—a business that matters on the level of God and the Universe and the Kingdom.

This isn't just about money or success. In the end, it's all about God.

So how is this idea of yours going to connect to God's plan?

Remember, this doesn't have to be about proclaiming your faith to every customer who walks in the door. There are tons of ways to incorporate God into your business idea. Chick-fil-A stays closed on Sundays to make sure everyone who works for them has a day off to "rest, spend time with family and friends, and worship if they choose to do so."

If you are in the mood to testify, you can do so in a way that doesn't cause offense or make customers uncomfortable. In-N-Out Burger, for instance, puts Bible verses on their cups and wrappers. Mary Kay Ash, who founded the cosmetics company Mary Kay, simply attributed all of her success to God in her biography.

But this really only scratches the surface. There are so many ways to make a difference in your business. God has a lot to say about giving people time off to rest in the Bible. He's also big on helping the less fortunate. You could bring God into your business simply by paying people vacation time or donating some of your profits to a charity.

You can refuse to use products at your business that are harmful to the environment or that involve child or slave labor.

You can choose to hire ex-felons or use some resources to help train the disabled in new work.

You can plant a tree for every sale.

You can donate leftover food or clothes to homeless shelters.

The options are nearly endless, but before you move forward with your idea, you should know which ones appeal to you, so you can incorporate them into your business as it develops.

CUTTING DOWN YOUR IDEAS

Every TV show you love starts out in a writers' room. That's where all the writers for the show—sometimes up to a couple dozen people—sit together and just come up with ideas. They take an initial concept of the show—three doctors learning the ropes as new members of the ER team—and build out stories. They think about what will happen over a whole season—Doctor One gets locked in a closet, Doctor Two has her first critically ill patient—and break it down into episodes. They introduce potential themes, side stories, and big revelations.

In that process, a whole lot of bad ideas are going to come out: story ideas that just don't work, jokes that don't land, plot twists that are too convoluted or don't shock anyone. Using the Splatter Approach, TV writers know putting the bad stuff out there is important because that's the only way you get to the good stuff. You throw it all up on the wall and whatever sticks: that's the show.

But that only works if you cut the bad stuff.

We've all seen movies with too many characters doing too much stuff to achieve too many goals. Those movies are always exhausting disappointments. So once you have thrown together all your potential Big Ideas, it's time to start making choices about what stays up on the board and what goes into the trash bin.

To start making those cuts, you can run your ideas through a filter to see what works and what doesn't. Filter everything until you can answer one particular question with one specific answer:

Which *one* idea of yours speaks to your purpose, looks like a success, and offers something no one else can?

To get to that answer, you should take advantage of the greatest tool humanity has ever developed: the internet.

To filter your ideas down to the one Big Idea that excites you, you've got to do research. So hop on Google and start checking out the competition.

If you have some potential Big Ideas about designing shoes, look into shoe companies. What makes a shoe company succeed? How do they differentiate themselves from each other? Which idea of yours fits the general mold but is different enough you could create a brand identity?

If your Big Ideas all revolve around opening a burger restaurant, look into the burger spots in your town. Visit each one of them. Read the reviews online. Why do people prefer one burger place over another? What is it about each place that keeps people coming back? And which idea of yours would make for a distinct, successful burger restaurant that can compete with the big chains?

Maybe you can invent a shoe made out of plastic from the ocean. Or maybe your burger place is known for serving the best plant-based patties around. There's no right answer here— it just has to be your answer.

FINDING A CUSTOMER

At this point, you should be close to your Big Idea. If not, that's alright. It took Michelangelo two years to sculpt David. It may take you more than the span of a chapter to come up with an idea that fulfills your purpose, plays into God's plans, and can be a success in the market.

Or, maybe you have five Big Ideas. Wonderful! Pick the one that feels most distinct, most likely to succeed, or the easiest to implement, and concentrate on that.

Once you have that one Big Idea, you finally have something concrete to work toward. You know what your purpose will look like! That is such an awesome accomplishment! Now you're not just going to be some type of baker but a baker who makes custom wedding cakes from their home. You're not just opening some kind of burger restaurant but the only exclusively vegan burger spot in town.

But now you have to ask yourself: who's going to buy this?

Having a great Big Idea isn't enough in business. You've got to figure out who your ideal customer is. Because you've got to start tailoring your Big Idea to them.

8

Who's Buying This?

During one of my summer trips to Naples, Florida, we stayed right next to the marina at Vanderbilt Beach. I loved that place. Looking out the window, I would watch all the big fishing boats coming in at the end of the day. Then, we'd head out to the dock to cast our own lines and try our luck at catching dinner.

This was a rather enterprising activity on my family's part. Those big ships would throw all their leftover bait overboard and chum the water. All we had to do was cast a line and wait for the big fish that swam into the marina for the feast to bite.

This was as easy as could be—basically child's play—but I still managed to make a mess of it.

I was just casting my line out into the water, letting it land wherever it might, and hoping to reel in something worth showing my dad. That lack of any focus and technique is probably why, one evening, I caught not a big fish or a little minnow or even a boot or old tire or something.

I caught a pelican.

That massive bird took the bait and the hook and the line and flew off into the sunset, leaving ten-year-old me with nothing but a rod and a funny story.

CHOOSING BAIT FOR THE RIGHT FISH

When you try to catch every fish, you can end up catching a pelican. When you try to speak to every customer, you end up speaking to no one.

Those are the rules we live by. Any time you try to be too broad—cast a wide net as it were—in what you say or what you do, you end up missing every target.

This is the wisdom in Jesus speaking to one group of people during his life. His message was tailored for them through the Scriptures, ancient Jewish culture, and the Roman world in that moment. It was left to His followers to adapt that message to each new "customer."

Churches often miss this lesson. They try to create a message that invites everyone inside—because everyone *is* welcome inside. But because they try to speak to every passerby, including the die-hard faithful, lapsed believers, Christianity-curious, conservatives, liberals, and moderates, they never actually attract anyone.

VOUS Church, where I attend, takes a different route. They send the congregation out into the community. That way, they get to know Miami and Miamians and can speak directly to various communities and their concerns.

Each message from VOUS may speak to a different person, but it's always speaking to *someone*. And somewhat paradoxically, once you're speaking to *someone*, it becomes a lot easier to speak to *everyone*.

This is how a business has to operate as well. To find the dedicated customer base that will allow you to start growing, you need to speak directly to them. And while you may eventually branch out to speaking to several different types of customers, you want to start by speaking directly to the people who will be most interested in what you're selling.

Defining this "ideal customer" can be almost absurdly specific. For instance, for *The Bible Study*, my ideal customer was a twenty-two-year-old woman who shops at Urban Outfitters, loves plants, has white walls in her room, listens to '90s hip-hop, and, of course, is a Christian who wants to get more from the Bible but feels intimidated by it. I called her Madison.

Just imagining Madison gave me clarity—about the type of language I should use in the book, how I should talk about *The*

Bible Study in advertising, and what the book should look like. I spent a lot of time finding a marble print for the cover of Part One and a sleek black-and-white for Part Two that looked like something you'd find on the bookshelf at a trendy bookstore.

And guess what? It worked.

We made a direct connection with that ideal audience. Twenty-two-year-old women like Madison bought the book in huge numbers. Then they shared it with friends. Then they bought it for their family members. And quickly, it became a phenomenon.

Speaking to an ideal customer is how you sneak your Big Idea into everyone's life. You go through the ideal customer to everyone else.

This technique is so powerful, you see it used by big companies every day.

Who was Geico trying to speak to with those caveman ads a few years ago? That was probably the same demographic as the Bud Light frogs from years past: young men who find those goofy ads appealing. That's not the same group Coca-Cola appeals to with its Christmas commercials: those are trying to speak to parents and their children.

Just think of the assumptions you make when you see a Ford F-150. Who do you think is driving that truck? I bet they're completely different from the person you assume drives a Subaru Crosstrek.

The source of these assumptions isn't the vehicle itself. They come out of what we've learned from who Ford and Subaru are trying to talk to in their commercials. Every F-150 ad has rugged guys driving over rugged terrain. Every Crosstrek ad has mothers driving their kids on vacation. And that's who ends up buying most of those vehicles.

That doesn't mean no mothers ever buy F-150s and no rugged guys drive Crosstreks. They sell those vehicles to all sorts of people, but there's one group in particular they talk to, and that gives those vehicles an identity people can grasp in a moment and know if it fits them.

You can—and should—do this with your Big Idea, too. Start watching commercials, visiting stores, and scanning ads with an eye on who exactly the company is trying to speak to. With a little practice, you'll pick up on the cues that make it as clear as if the name of the audience were written across the top of the page.

Then you can replicate those cues in your own communication with your ideal customer.

WHO NEEDS WHAT *YOU'RE* SELLING?

There are more than seven billion unique individuals on this planet of ours, and I'm sure you can see your Big Idea appealing to almost all of them. So how do you determine who your ideal customer actually *is*?

How do you find your Madison?

Sometimes, this is easy. If you want to design clothes for young professional men interested in the latest trends in Europe, you already know who your customer is—the Big Idea is already *tailored* to them. But this is often a little more complicated than choosing who your suits fit.

Let's say you want to open a coffee shop. Who do you want to come into your coffee shop? Everyone!

But *everyone* isn't a customer. You need someone you can talk to directly.

To determine who that someone is, go back to the research you were doing in the last chapter. Back then, I told you to visit all the competition in the area—in this case, coffee shops.

Look at their website and their social media accounts. Who do they seem to be speaking to, and what customer groups do they seem to attract? It doesn't have to be just one group, but there are probably some broad generalizations you can make about who is in there.

Starbucks brings in the young professionals and middle-aged women, for instance. A quick scan inside will show those groups make up most of the people in line. Maybe that's all your area has. Or maybe there's another coffee shop where a lot of the parents go when the kids are in school, and another that has a bit of a stuffy, intellectual vibe with books on every shelf and Chopin tinkling along in the background.

If these coffee shops are already established, you probably don't want to start out competing directly with them for the same customers.

So who is your coffee shop going to speak to?

Well, who is being left out of this conversation? And who among those being left out would really enjoy your Big Idea?

If your Big Idea is to connect your love of music and love of coffee together with a live music café, you might want to start trying to attract the eye of the hipsters in your community. You could also have a secondary audience of older jazzheads with nowhere to hear those blaring trumpets in the evening.

Alternatively, maybe your coffee shop is going to focus on ethical practices and the best espresso in the state—offering a place where everyone can come in and have a great cup of coffee and feel good about themselves. Then your ideal customer may be someone in their twenties who is focused on the environment or social justice...or wishes they were.

Go back to what makes your Big Idea stand out and think of the people most interested in that idea. That's your ideal customer. Now all you have to do is find a way to talk to them.

MAKE THEM REAL

The trick to building a business around an ideal customer is to make your company feel personal.

Bring your generic customer to life.

Put flesh and bones on their profile by giving them a name, an age, and a gender.

Decide if they're married and have kids.

Give them an income, interests, social media platform preferences, sports teams they support, artists they love, podcasts they listen to.

Write down what their internal frustrations are and the parts of their life they take the most pride in.

Determine what gives them meaning in life. What is their purpose, and how might it resonate with yours?

Get specific enough that you'd recognize them on the street.

You don't want to make this up out of nowhere. Observe people who fit the general profile and draw conclusions from them. If you're trying to get those twenty-something hipsters in your coffee shop, talk to some twenty-something hipsters and find out what their lives are like. What are they excited about? What are they worried about these days? What makes them turn their heads, stop in their tracks, and walk into a new store?

And try to have fun with this. This is one of the most creative parts of the job!

You're designing the hero of the story you are going to tell through your Big Idea. You're going to link your business to their hero journey and show them that they can be so much more if they wear your shoes or visit your gym.

This is storytelling.

It's art.

It's creation.

And what could be more godly than that?

But this only works if that story reflects a reality. You aren't selling fiction here, you're selling a certain truth to your customer. And if you want them to believe in your Big Idea, you have to believe in it too—all the way to your core.

9

What's at Your Core?

There are plenty of companies that sell jackets and backpacks, and many of them are pretty affordable. So what makes people buy Patagonia?

It all comes down to what Patagonia stands for. Namely, the environment. They're outspoken about their desire to protect the outdoors, going so far as to give 1 percent of their sales revenue to environmental groups. They also regularly use their platform to push for land preservation.

They lay out their core values as:

Build the best product

Cause no unnecessary harm

Use business to protect nature

Not bound by convention

All of the values add up to a company built on conservation, quality, and a little bit of edge. So when people spend extra on a Patagonia fleece or a duffel bag, they aren't looking particularly at the price tag. They're buying into a way of looking at the world that they agree with. They are expressing agreement in those values with their purchase.

They have certain core values, and they shop those values—even when it costs a bit extra.

THE VALUE OF CORE VALUES

At The Brand Sunday, we have three core values:

Help People Grow: Our main purpose as a company is to make it easier for people to understand the Bible and to grow in their relationship with God. That's what we are here for.

Be Excellent: In everything we do and everything we create, we want it to be done to the best of our ability. This is why we focus so much on the details.

Be Generous: We know that none of our success is possible without God's hand on it, so we strive for over-the-top generosity with our finances, time, and wisdom.

Whenever a customer reads those values, they know something real about us. And if they agree with those values, they're more eager to purchase from us because they know their money is going to the right place. It's going to a project that matters.

Grounding your company in the right values allows you not only to speak clearly to your ideal customer but to guide your business according to your personal values.

At Chick-fil-A, founder Truett Cathy built the business from 1946 onward based on his Southern Baptist beliefs. That's why the restaurant is still closed on Sundays.

When Tom Chappell, founder of Tom's of Maine, was at Harvard Divinity School, one of his professors told him to treat his business like a ministry. Tom took his advice and put the concept into his mission statement, which is, "to help create a better world by exchanging our faith, experiences, and hope."

What do all of these values have in common? They are clearly defined, get to the core of what each business is about, and speak to the deep devotion each entrepreneur has to God and creation.

These core values don't have to be outward facing. You don't have to share them with a single customer. They can be something to drive your business, your employees, or even just you. And you don't have to explicitly talk about God as your partner either.

But the essence of your relationship with your customer and God should be in your values. And that should come through in everything you do.

DEVELOPING YOUR CORE

Patagonia's ideal customer is a rugged, adventurous, icono-clastic environmentalist who likes to look good, and their core values match that customer.

That's not to say the values were constructed for the customer, but it's important that there is overlap.

Luckily, core values often flow directly out of what you already know about your business. You've built a Big Idea around a God-given purpose that stands out from the rest through the particular interests of you and your ideal customer. And you have plans to make that business matter by connecting to the causes you are most passionate about.

So all the ingredients necessary to create core values are there. You just have to spell them out.

To make this concise, think about why you're doing this in the first place. You were made to be an entrepreneur who partners with God. Why are you choosing to follow that purpose in this way?

There's no single answer to this question, and you don't have to have a single core value. But there may be a few things you want to include.

If you want to make the best handmade ice cream in your city, that's a value.

So is donating some of that ice cream to the local children's hospital to give those kids a little joy.

If you care about reforesting the planet while introducing the world to the best vegan food they'll ever taste, those are some great values to put down in writing.

The important thing here is to link your Big Idea with your passion to make your business matter. Essentially, you're spelling out your purpose here. And once you have that in words, it can drive you forward and drive customers to you.

YOU HAVE TO LIVE YOUR VALUES

The reason Patagonia remains such a dominant company in their space is because they don't just claim to care about the environment—they live up to it. Despite the fact that their stances cost them money and probably alienate some potential customers, they repeatedly recommit to those values.

In other words, they walk the walk.

At The Brand Sunday, we try to do the same. We run every decision through the lens of our core values. We constantly ask ourselves:

How is this going to help people?

Does this live up to our high standards?

Are we giving enough?

We live in a cynical age when people don't trust the government, companies, or even their own neighbors. They consider everyone in business to be in it solely for money.

You are different. Your company will be different.

But you have to prove that by living up to your values.

If you claim to care about workers, you can't put your employees on minimum wage to increase your profits or skip the fair trade option for the cheaper product made with slave labor somewhere in the world.

This makes business a little harder, but it also makes you stand out.

People pay more to shop at Patagonia because it's one of the few companies they trust to do the right thing. People will drive out of their way to get Chick-fil-A not just because it's delicious—it's so delicious!—but because they know the company lives up to its values.

People will treat your company the same way, but only if you prove to them that you mean what you say.

And only, as we're about to see, if you can say what you mean in the right way.

10

Finding Your *Logos*

The author and executive Seth Godin once said that people don't buy goods and services. They buy "relations, stories, and magic."

The founders of Warby Parker clearly agree. In theory, they could just tell their customers that they sell good, cheap prescription glasses, but that wouldn't be nearly as impressive as the story behind the company.

It all started when one of the founders lost his glasses on a trip in grad school. The cost of replacing those glasses was so high he went an entire semester without replacing them. Together with his future co-founders, they looked into the source of the expense and decided they wanted to develop a way to offer better, cheaper glasses to the world.

It's a good story.

And the story is the point.

The fact is, you can have an incredible Big Idea, but if you don't have an incredible story that appeals to your customers, you'll struggle to find much success. So if you want to build that business that matters, you have to build a story to explain it.

HUMANS CRAVE STORIES

Have you ever read the theologian Thomas Aquinas? Me neither. I know he's an important figure—the most famous Christian philosopher of the Middle Ages, even!—and there's undoubtedly plenty of value to be gained by reading him, but who has the time for all that dense medieval philosophy?

There's a reason big tomes of philosophy tend to sit on the shelf gathering dust while you can't keep your hands off the latest Bob Goff or Max Lucado. It's the same reason most nonfiction, religious, and self-help books are filled with anecdotes and narratives.

People love a good story.

This is something that runs deep in our nature. Humans have craved stories from the very beginning. Stories are how we make sense of our lives—down to how we construct what happened to us during the day—and our place in the world.

This is why the Bible was written as God's *story* and not a list of God's expectations and explanations. Crack open any book—

yes, even those dense law books in the Torah like Leviticus and Deuteronomy—and you'll find a story.

It didn't have to be this way. Some early gospel efforts that didn't make it into the Bible imagined God's book in a far different light. Most famously, the Gospel of Thomas just included a list of sayings from Jesus. Nothing about His birth, His life, His mission, or His death. Just His words—plus a lot of stuff He probably didn't say. It's not nearly as compelling as what we have at the front of the New Testament. God designed us to crave stories, and He designed His book to speak to us through stories. He uses stories to connect us to Him.

And you need to use stories to connect customers to you.

This is why Warby Parker doesn't just give you a list of statistics to prove their glasses are cheaper than their competitors'. Numbers just don't pack the same punch as a narrative that shows why they make sure they have the cheapest specs on the market.

WHAT IS YOUR STORY?

If you aren't a writer, coming up with a story can be a bit daunting. But this isn't so hard once you give it a bit of thought. In fact, you already have the start of your story in the core values you developed in the last chapter. When you develop a story to tell people who you are, you want those values to come through.

Warby Parker starts their story like this:

"Warby Parker was founded with a rebellious spirit and a lofty objective: to offer designer eyewear at a revolutionary price, while leading the way for socially conscious businesses."

See how those values lead right into their story? You want your customer to be able to look at your core values and your story and see one whole, clear image of who you are and what you stand for.

Your values are a great start to your story! Now you're ready to really build that narrative!

Solve the Problem

Once you have your values grounded in your story, you can start building the story by telling your customer why they're there.

Basically, what problem are you solving? And why are you the person to solve it?

At Warby Parker, the problem is the need for affordable prescription glasses.

At The Brand Sunday, we know that people want to grow in their relationship with God. In order to do that, they need to understand the Bible better. The problem is that seems like such a big task, which can be overwhelming. We think it should be easier, so we simplify things for them.

Our story has to tell our customers why they should trust us with such an important issue. So our story has to include my own false starts in reading the Bible.

You've already identified the problems you can solve in Chapter 7. At this point, you just want to add that to your story. If you're opening a hair salon, why should people come to you instead of a competitor? What is it in your story that lets them know you understand their needs better than anyone else?

Make It Personal

A good story requires more than a problem; it takes personality—or rather, it takes personal stakes. This is mostly a tweak on your problem. It has to feel like the people at your company personally understand what the customer is going through.

You can trust Warby Parker because the founders lived through a semester without glasses. They understand the struggle! When I was developing *The Bible Study*, I kept coming back to how much I wished I'd had this resource when I was twenty-two. If I'd understood the Bible better back then, I would have been in a completely different place in my life by the time I was twenty-six and having a crisis in my car outside of Starbucks.

I'd gone through years of business failures and pushed away some of the most valuable parts of my life—my friends, the

Christian community—and it was only once I dove into the Bible that I found my God-given purpose.

That was my story, and it was personal.

At heart, your story should show the customer why this business matters to *you*. If you open a handcrafted furniture business, what is it that made you so invested in that project? Were you always drawn to comfortable, well-made furniture? Were the skills passed down through your family? Did you break your arm when a cheap chair broke under you?

Your story doesn't have to be overcomplicated. This is your purpose! You're partnering with God to make the world a better place! Just tell people about that.

Fundamentally, your story has to come from a place of honesty. It has to feel personal because you're trying to prove to the reader that your story isn't manufactured corporate gibberish. It means something, just like your business.

Make Them Feel Something

Once you have the personal side of your problem in your story, you're almost done. You're just missing one ingredient: a little feeling.

Think back to a book you read ten years ago and really enjoyed but haven't read since. What do you remember about it? You probably remember some fragments of the plot and a bit about the characters. What's-his-name decided he had to join the fight and met what's-her-name after the battle, and there was a big tragic ending.

One thing you almost certainly remember much more clearly is how that book made you *feel*.

I cried for days.

I was in a funk for a week.

I kept wishing the book would go on forever.

Long after we forget the details, we remember the feeling of the stories we encounter. We remember the joy, the humor, the terror, and the sadness of a story because they make a far deeper impression on us.

As you polish your story, you should aim to leave the customer feeling something—uplifted, hopeful, even angry sometimes.

You might even want them to feel a combination of those feelings. You can feel angry that some people have to go without glasses and hopeful that Warby Parker is going to help change that. You can feel fear that the environment is dying and excited that some young enterprising person is opening a plant-based burger spot in town.

Long after you forget the details of Warby Parker's story, you'll remember how it made you feel. And you'll feel it all over again when you see those glasses online or in a store.

GET THE LANGUAGE RIGHT

Shepard Fairey is one of my favorite muralists. You've definitely seen his work. He made one of the most famous posters of all time. It was a picture of former President Barack Obama with one word underneath it: "Hope."

Sometimes, all it takes to say something right is one word. Sometimes, it takes 783,137—the total number of words in the King James Bible, the first official English translation.

In either case, the same lesson applies: words matter.

This is why God puts such importance on His name. Don't take it in vain—because His name matters! It's the reason Jesus Christ is the Word in the Gospel of John.

The word for Word is actually quite fascinating in itself. We've already met the Greek word *logos*, but it doesn't just refer to how God speaks to us. It also refers to reason—it's where we get "logic." In certain ancient Greek philosophical traditions, it also stands for the principle that generates the entire universe.

I know that sounds familiar.

Calling Jesus the "Word," then, was clearly a good use of language.

Language is a major concern of God and the Biblical authors because it's important to get your language right when you are trying to communicate an important message to people, whether that message is "Jesus is Lord" or "you should come to my store."

That's not to say that every word is all that important. A lot of emphasis is often put on business names, but there's not a ton of evidence that a business name actually makes much difference. Consider the names of some of the most successful and valuable companies in the world:

Apple

Microsoft

Google

Walmart

Johnson & Johnson

None of those names scream for your attention. And God obviously doesn't put much emphasis on this either. After all, Bible just means "book" in Greek. God didn't even give it a title!

So instead of sweating over a business name, focus on the language of your story.

And the first principle of getting your story language right is to keep it simple and direct. StoryBrand cautions, "If you confuse, you lose." I love that.

This lesson doesn't just apply to marketing. Journalists are told to write at a level even a middle schooler can understand.

And Albert Einstein himself suggested, "If you can't explain it to a six-year-old, you probably don't understand it yourself."

So keep a few basic writing rules in mind as you craft your story. Never use a big, complicated word when a short, easily understood word would do. Never write a paragraph when you can say it in a sentence. And keep your sentences short and easy to follow.

Words are also important when trying to give your story that emotional impact. There's a reason "it was a dark and stormy night" feels like such a great first sentence. "Dark" and "stormy" give us a certain emotional feeling that makes us feel a little tense. We know something thrilling is about to happen.

This is also why that Obama poster worked so well, whether you agreed with his policies or not. Few words immediately fill us with the calming sense that it is all going to be alright better than the word "hope."

MAKING YOUR STORY VISUAL

Words are only one part of what makes a successful business story. To make those words stand out and get noticed, you need to back them up with a design that captures people's eye, interest, and respect.

Remember those websites you visited in early internet days that looked cheap and poorly put together? The ones with bright green backgrounds that made the text hard to read and the blurry images? How inspired would you be to buy from one of those websites today?

Shepard Fairey's Obama poster didn't just work because the word "hope" so perfectly encapsulated how people felt about a man running for office, it had *a look* that somehow also captured the mood of the moment.

Take a look at competitors in your industry. What sort of choices do they make in the colors and images they use on their websites, billboards, and storefronts? Why do you think these super successful businesses made those choices?

They found a combination that spoke to their ideal customers, and they built a brand around it.

This is why *The Bible Study* looks the way it does. As I mentioned before, we designed everything—the book, the website, the emails, the advertising—to appeal to those trendy young Christians who wanted to get closer to Jesus.

Design is so important because, just like words, visual images inspire emotions. We can see this just by taking a spin around the color wheel.

Red fills us with passionate emotions, from anger to intense love.

Yellow is joyful like the sun.

Orange is a warm color that feels playful and creative.

Green is fresh as spring.

Blue is calming as the sea.

And purple gives a sense of luxury.

Meanwhile, black is powerful and modern.

And brown suggests the ground below us.

It's not hard to understand why Starbucks would use green in its logo to suggest something fresh and refreshing while McDonald's fills children with intense joy with those bright reds and yellows.

Obviously, these visual elements aren't always easy to come up with on your own. It takes a certain artistic eye for the right font for your website or the right creative twist on an image to make your logo.

If this isn't your strength, you can hire these decisions out to design experts. There are a lot of great designers out there, from agencies to freelance artists. With so many options, you can almost certainly find someone to do great work that fits your aesthetics at a price that fits your budget.

One thing you definitely shouldn't do, though, is shrug these choices off. You don't want to end up with one of those bright green, hideous websites. There's no way a customer will stick around long enough to really get to know you.

LAUNCHING YOUR BIG IDEA

With the core values from the last chapter, a killer story about you and your company, and the right visual designs, you will have all the elements you need to build a brand around your Big Idea.

At this point, you've accomplished all the creative work necessary to create a successful business that matters.

Now you've just got to launch it.

A launch can make all the difference in the success of your Big Idea. That means you want to get this right.

So let's start the countdown and get this Big Idea airborne.

Part IV

Ready for Launch

11

Start the Countdown

In days gone by, if you had a Big Idea, your options were basically limited to taking out a huge loan to open a brick-and-mortar store or selling your idea to a bigger company. The first option came with a ton of debt and risk; the second option didn't really allow you to live your purpose. You would do all the work, pitch the product, and exchange control of your idea for a nice payday.

If you tried to go it alone, you had limited options to build interest in your Big Idea. TV ads were usually too expensive; newspaper ads might not reach enough people. You just had to open the doors and hope word of mouth was strong enough to keep you in business.

Thankfully, we aren't living in that era anymore.

Modern technology allows you to connect directly with your customers and open almost any kind of business at far less cost.

But with all that new promise, there's a lot more competition. That means entrepreneurs have a new responsibility: getting the launch right.

A big launch can transform your Big Idea into an industry power player almost overnight. How much of a power player? Ever heard of Casper mattresses, or Native Deodorant, or Dollar Shave Club, or Harry's, or Warby Parker? All of those companies were just ideas before a big launch transformed them into multimillion-dollar household brands.

WHAT IS A LAUNCH?

It's no exaggeration that a launch can set the trajectory for your entire business future. Get it right, and you're the next Warby Parker. Get it wrong, and you're onto the next Big Idea in a year's time.

The stakes are pretty high, then. You want to get this right. But what, exactly, are you trying to get right?

A business launch is your introduction to the world. These days, you don't just throw open the doors and hope for business. Nor do you try to get business customer by customer and hope that snowballs into success.

Instead, you throw a big, fancy opening with trumpets blaring, spotlights streaming through the sky, and streamers wafting through the air.

Imagine what it must have been like when the circus came to small towns a hundred years ago: the excitement, the paradise, the noise! That's what you're going for.

Only you're basically doing it all online.

THE LAUNCH CODE

So if you can't call in the marching band or afford those spotlights, how are you going to launch your business successfully?

There are numerous pieces you need to put in place for a successful launch. These don't have to be extremely expensive, but they do require some investment of your time and money.

You'll need a team of smart, reliable people in place before you open.

You'll need to put your business online so you can connect with potential customers and let everyone get to know you—scary as that may seem.

You'll need tools in place to turn that interest into future sales.

And you'll need to organize everything around the big bash: a launch week that converts all your efforts into your first sales.

When I say that it takes a lot to launch a business, I mean it.

It's a lot.

But you can do this. With the advice ahead, you can find the right people, create an online presence, transfer that interest into real customers, and create a launch that sets your business off for a future of dizzying success.

You can be the next Warby Parker. You can be the next Apple!

You just need to get the details right.

12

Building a Team

Jesus Christ was the Son of God, but He wasn't the one
to share that fact with most of the world. His following during
His life was relatively small. We know He had at least a few
thousand people interested in what He had to say, but most of
those were the casual, curious crowd, and all of them were con-
fined to one nation.

Most likely, the number of true believers at His death was
shockingly small—we're talking the population of a small
suburban neighborhood.

If that had been the sum of His influence after the resurrection,
Christianity would be at best a small regional religion. More
likely, it never would have made it out of the first century. But
Christianity isn't a relic of the Roman Empire. It's the biggest
religion in the world—with more than two billion followers
today.

What made the difference?

His team.

Jesus saved us, but His team spread the word of salvation. That small group of devoted followers spread across the Roman world until every town knew the name of Jesus Christ and what His sacrifice meant for all humanity.

To achieve His purpose, God's only Son died alone for our sins. To share His message, He needed a team.

THE VALUE OF A TEAM

Rare is the business that requires only one employee. Business is simply too complex to be handled alone. As you head toward launch, you need experienced people with expertise in everything from social media to shipping.

You aren't going to do this all on your own. So you have to choose your team carefully.

To begin, let's go back to a basic principle of business we learned in Chapter 3: double down on your strengths. In business, you don't have to be great at everything. You just have to really dig into what you do well and hire out the rest.

In general, if you're great at something in business, stick with it. If you're good at it, do it until you can afford to pay someone else to do it. And if you're bad at it, hire someone to do it now.

At The Brand Sunday, I started out doing everything I was capable of. I wrote and designed the book. I was decent at marketing, so I handled that at first, too. But I had no idea how to deal with manufacturing or distribution—those were skills and resources far outside my capabilities—so I hired those needs out.

Over time, though, I began outsourcing more roles. I brought in a freelance designer to redesign *The Bible Study* cover to cover. Then, I brought in a marketing organization to boost our marketing reach and success—and oh man did they boost it.

At this point, The Brand Sunday now has four in-house employees, including Gisela, who runs social media and shoots some of our video content; Caleb, our COO who focuses on everyday business and our growth; and Bree, who runs our admin, customer service, and editing work. I'm number four.

We also have a robust team of freelancers we work with— including Katlyn, who does our design work, and Paul, who does all our photos and videos—a marketing agency called Activ, distribution partners in Tristan Publishing, an accountant, and a trademark attorney.

It's a strong team in which each person brings different skills and different expertise into the business. And it works. At this point, I couldn't run The Brand Sunday without each of these people by my side.

HOW TO ASSEMBLE YOUR TEAM

I didn't start out with a team. It was two years before I hired my first employee—Bree, who came on as a part-time admin employee. Like most businesses, I had significant needs to set up a good launch, and I had very little money to pay for them. It was not an easy position to be in.

But there was a way through for me—and the same strategies I used to build a team will work for you. It all comes down to hiring well in the right type of roles and doing a bit of creative accounting.

Outsource Roles

Some businesses will require staff right away. If you're opening a restaurant, you need servers and chefs from day one. But many businesses do not require a single full-time employee for years. If that applies to your company, the place to start is with freelancers and agencies.

You'd be amazed by how many jobs you can outsource at many companies.

You can hire out people to handle all your media—including video and photos—website development, and social media ad strategy.

You can hire freelance copywriters to write all your marketing and website content.

You can hire artists to design logos.

And bookkeepers to keep your finances in order.

Outsourcing distribution leaves the issues of packaging, storing, and shipping your product in the hands of professionals.

And a quick stop at a trademark attorney covers your copyrights and trademarks.

And this is really just the beginning.

When starting out, you can outsource almost any role in an online business.

Even brick-and-mortar businesses can benefit from some of these outsourcing options. Coffee shops can outsource media and marketing. They can outsource bean roasting. And they can outsource food to a local bakery, potentially adding another incentive to customers to come in. If they sell merchandise, they can outsource designs and production for tote bags, shirts, French presses, and more.

In the end, they may be able to run the whole place with hardly an employee in sight.

Hire the Right People

Just because outsourcing is easy doesn't mean you should choose the first name that pops up for a role. Remember, you're hiring to cover your weaknesses, so the best thing you can do is hire people who are really strong where you are weak.

Everyone you hire should be smarter than you in the area they work.

As Elon Musk put it, "Don't confuse schooling with education. I didn't go to Harvard, but the people that work for me did."

To do this right, you might have to overcome a little ego. Recognize your own limitations and celebrate where others excel.

Look at their experience and past projects, and don't be afraid to pick the person who shines most.

Of course, all that talent and knowledge only goes so far if you don't work well with this person. Even if you only talk over email and on an occasional call, you want to enjoy working with this person. Having people you like and who like you at your business makes everyone happier and more productive.

And don't forget your values. In a business like mine, it's crucial that those who work for us believe Jesus is Lord, but that is certainly not the case for many businesses. Whether you hire Christians or not, you want those you work with to share the values of your company. If you run a coffee shop, you don't want to hire a barista who hates coffee or believes no one should ingest caffeine. And you don't want someone working as a manager who places maximizing profits ahead of doing what matters in your business. If they'd rather buy cheap beans because fair trade is too expensive, they probably aren't in the right place.

By now, you have your core values set and know your lines in the sand for your business. Make sure no hires cross them, even if they fit every other need. Those lines will ensure your business matters in the end.

Paying for Your Team

Employee or freelance, your biggest concern is probably a little more basic:

How are you going to afford all these hires?

Money is tight when you start out, and it always seems like you need more than you can pay for—and your team is no different. Luckily, there are a ton of ways to make your money fit the need.

Your options start with technology. Every day, there seems to be a new app, service, or e-commerce solution to lower your costs.

After COVID, just about everyone knows the value of Zoom tele-conferences, but if you're starting out, you may not realize how much that simple invention could save you in office costs. At The Brand Sunday, we don't even have an office. We Zoom or Slack most of the time. If we need to meet up, we find a corner in a Starbucks to chat or, at most, we rent an office through WeWork.

That completely removes the cost of office real estate and also allows us to hire employees and freelancers from anywhere in the world. If the best employee at the right cost lives in Alaska or the Bahamas, there's no difficulty in bringing them on board.

This is far more cost-effective than the traditional labor model.

You may also find some flexibility in working out a barter with service providers rather than paying in cash. There may be local photographers and videographers who would trade a few hours of work for a month of free coffee at your café, a chance to put some of their art up in your store, or free access to your app. A marketer may work for a percentage of your first-year revenue.

You might also be able to trade like-for-like services. For example, if you're developing a new online accounting business and need someone to develop the technology, you could trade tax work for tech work.

And potentially get that crucial business service that can make all the difference when you launch.

BECOME A LEADER

By combining freelance work, online solutions, and potential non-monetary compensation, you can find a creative way to put all the team pieces together for your business before you actually launch. Bringing the pieces together isn't enough, though. Jesus didn't just find twelve decent apostles and let them figure out God's message.

He had to lead them.

Leadership can be a real challenge for new entrepreneurs. After all, being a creative person with a God-given purpose in business doesn't necessarily translate to being a leader of men. But a leader you must be all the same.

So what does good leadership look like? And how do you replicate it?

This isn't as tough as it may seem. For instance, you probably already have expectations for yourself and your business—reflected in the values you defined. A big part of leadership is just communicating those expectations and values and making sure people live up to them. To keep expectations reasonable, you want to have an open dialogue with those you bring on board.

Ask your videographer what a successful video project looks like.

Ask your website developer how long it takes to design your site and get it online.

Get your marketer to ballpark how many customers they can bring in on the budget you give them.

Then, all you have to do is get people to stick to those numbers.

Easy, right?

Sometimes.

If you've hired well, you don't have to constantly micromanage your team. You can answer questions, give feedback, and focus on your own responsibilities, instead. Assuming everyone delivers as promised, pat yourself on the back for your successful leadership.

However, if targets aren't hit, or if a better option comes along, good leadership requires you to make some tough choices. At The Brand Sunday, we had a great printing partner in Canada for our first run of *The Bible Study*. But we found a lower-cost option with the same quality elsewhere. It was my job as the leader to tell our printer we were going elsewhere.

You have to give yourself permission to make the best choices for your business. When someone is a bad fit, has a different vision, or lacks the focus, it's okay to look elsewhere.

These choices are never comfortable, but they are necessary. They're also, usually, pretty infrequent. Again, hiring well means you have to switch out people less frequently, and you can focus on the more pleasant aspects of leadership more often.

TRUST YOUR TEAM

There's a real Golden Rule element to leadership. You want to create a company that stands for kindness, empathy, and positivity because this company has to matter on a divine scale. But if you want your company to *have* those qualities and to *project* those qualities, you have to *display* them first yourself.

Be encouraging.

Give positive feedback.

Offer everyone love, compassion, and generosity.

And create a culture of trust.

Trust is an essential ingredient in a healthy team. If you trust others to do excellent work and let them do it in the way they feel is best, most people will repay that trust with better work and more loyalty.

When leading your team, always remember that this business is not just *your* calling. Your business is both your God-given purpose and a vehicle for dozens of people to fulfill *their* purpose by helping you complete your mission.

When Jesus called His apostles, He fulfilled His purpose by enabling them to fulfill theirs. He was called to die for our sins, and they were called to be fishers of men and spread the word. The mission could only succeed if everyone was able to do their part fully.

The only way the message could spread was if Jesus trusted those men to testify on His behalf.

The stakes are not as high at your business, but you have your own "Good News" to share, and you'll share it much more successfully if everyone on your team is given the room to do their best for God, for themselves, and for you.

13

Creating an Online Presence

A major reason the Good News spread across the world comes down to one man: Paul of Tarsus. While Jesus sent His Twelve out to testify, they limited their work to sharing the gospel with their fellow Jews. It was Paul, the new kid on the block, who took the message and spoke to the wider world.

To share this radical new idea that the Son of the One God had just died for everyone's sins, he went to where the people were, which in those days was the agora. The agora was the center of city life—something like a mix of street market, art museum, schoolyard, and debate center. Amid the people haggling over the price of dates, philosophers would stand around and shout their ideas to all who would listen.

That's where Paul went to change the world through the story of Jesus Christ.

But how did he do it? How did he manage to get anyone's attention in this loud, crowded, busy marketplace? And how did he manage to convince people that a man they had never heard about in a region they'd never visited had changed the cosmic game forever?

He connected the Word to the cultural world of his listeners.

He spoke in a language and used references people understood.

He introduced himself through connections to people those citizens already knew.

You all know Prisca and Aquila, right? Well, they swear by me and everything I'm about to say, so listen up.

Paul was an inspired genius in many ways, but perhaps it was his natural skills as a marketer that made it possible for him to have such an impact. He took an event that happened far away and spoke about it in a way that the people of Rome or Corinth could understand and relate to.

Two thousand years later, we're still trying to do the same thing. When I started marketing *The Bible Study* in preparation for my launch, I went to the most popular platform for my ideal customer: Instagram, the agora of millennials. I tried to take all of my ideas and make them as Instagrammable and shareable as possible.

It was only by standing in their marketplace and speaking their language that I could manage to get a few people to hear me over all the noise. And once they heard, it turned out a whole lot of them were interested.

OVERCOMING YOUR "FEAR OF MAN"

You probably know you'll need to be online to connect with your customers. Our entire lives are lived online. So what's keeping you from setting up social media pages for your new business?

Most likely, it's fear.

And a very particular type of fear.

This isn't fear of failure like we've covered already—or not quite. What keeps entrepreneurs from getting online and shouting about their amazing Big Ideas is what we call "the fear of man."

In the Bible, the fear of man refers to our need for approval from our fellow humans and our fear of criticism. Fear is a powerful force. So powerful, in fact, it can make entrepreneurs avoid the most potent source of connection with their potential customers in the history of the world.

Have you ever thought about opening a social media account, starting a website, or posting your thoughts online only to back out at the last second? What was going through your mind when you deleted that post you were working on?

What will people say?

What if nobody likes it?

What if they make fun of me?

That's the fear of man in action.

If you've ever struggled with the fear of man, I have some bad news for you:

You're going to have to get over it.

You are going to have to start using the internet to your advantage, and when you do, you will see your posts ignored or mocked. You will be called names. And some of it will be nasty.

Whether you have two hundred or two million followers, you will attract trolls who want to put you down.

Even early on, before *The Bible Study* became a real success, people—most of them were fellow Christians!—would post some very hurtful things in my comments. They questioned my faith. They questioned my authority. One person even called me Satan. Like, what?!

Here's the good news: "The fear of man lays a snare, but whoever trusts in the Lord is safe." That's Proverbs 29:25. That's what I always told myself. This is my calling. I am influencing people's lives. I am doing something that *matters* to God. Doing something that matters on the cosmic level is always going to upset the demonic powers, but God is going to see me through.

After all, this is what we signed up for. We are part of the team that will help Christ, in the words of John, "destroy the works of the devil." Since the beginning of Christianity, one rule has always been true:

When you take a stand with Jesus, you are going to get pushback.

I don't mean to imply any of my fellow brothers and sisters in Christ are demonic, only that these incredible tools we use—the computer, the internet, the smartphone—have a way of bringing out a terrible side in all of us. We have all seen how social media can invite the very worst in us to come out. The internet makes it easier to judge others, easier to say the most hurtful, cruel things we can imagine, and easier to ignore the humanity of those on the other side of the conversation.

Instead of allowing these assaults to get to me—and thus discourage me from my purpose—I reframed my feelings about those posts. Growing up, anytime I was picked on, my mom used to tell me, "They're only saying that because they're jealous." That's how I approach such comments now. I try to feel empathy toward those making them. There's something lacking in their life that makes them angry. They have so much anger, they want to hurt others. I can only hope that God heals their hearts, and they move on.

I know that I am on a path for something great—and you are there with me. We are fulfilling our God-given purpose in sharing a business that means something to the world—and giving up doesn't just hurt us, it hurts everyone.

Just consider what happened to movie director David Lean. By the late '60s, Lean was undoubtedly one of the greatest directors of all time. *Great Expectations, Lawrence of Arabia, Bridge over the River Kwai, Doctor Zhivago*: he had made some of the all-time great films. Then, he made a movie called *Ryan's Daughter*—and the critics hated it.

They didn't stop at just recommending people skip it; they mocked it mercilessly. That bothered Lean so much, he flew to New York to talk to some of his most vicious critics face-to-face. The result was a two-hour lunch over which they tore his film apart all over again.

Lean didn't direct for another fifteen years.

That's a sad story for David Lean, but it's far sadder for the rest of us. We missed out on fifteen years' worth of great movies because the fear of man kept Lean out of the director's chair.

Instead of facing such attacks like Lean, we have to aspire to be more like Walt Disney. When Disney was fired from the *Kansas City Star*, his editor told him he lacked imagination.

Can you believe that?

The man who is almost synonymous with imagination was told he simply didn't have what it takes.

Instead of hiding away, though, Disney made straight for LA, where he became, well, *Walt Disney*.

Anyone trying to build something that matters publicly will face a similar test.

We simply have to accept it as part of our mission. Paul was berated, beaten, and thrown in prison. We will face angry comments, accusations, and mockery.

Instead of hiding from it, accept it, and protect yourself by keeping those who know your value and believe in your purpose close, so that their words are the ones that you feel most deeply.

FIRST IMPRESSIONS MATTER

Once you overcome your fear of man and decide to share your Big Idea with the world, you have to start thinking about how you want to present that idea, and as I learned from world-renowned chef Gavin Kaysen, when it comes to presentation, the details matter.

I worked for chef Gavin for a year at two of his restaurants: Spoon & Stable and the now-closed Bellecour. When I say he taught me that details matter, I mean he taught me that the details are everything. His focus on them changed the way I view hospitality, work, and life in general.

Chef Gavin made sure every guest was met with a warm greeting by name as soon as they walked in the door of one of his restaurants. The smells of the kitchen wafted over to the entrance, and everyone knew they were in a special place. The staff is trained to make each moment memorable. And they do. That's why people keep coming back, and the awards keep piling up.

The value of this kind of service can't be overstated. Often, a business only gets one chance to make an impression. And a good first impression can be a magical thing that makes your business.

Like the first time Gisela saw snow. She grew up in South Florida and Puerto Rico, and the only snow she'd ever seen was in the movies. Then, last winter, we flew up to Minneapolis. There, in the parking lot outside of the hotel, was a huge pile of snow. The winter-hardened Midwesterner in me didn't even notice, but Gisela ran right for it and jumped in, laughing the entire time.

Magical was the only word for it.

But what does Gavin's focus on excellence or my wife's first snowman have to do with your business?

As you set out to speak in your agora, that first impression you make on people will matter.

Someone on Instagram or Google encounters thousands of ads, blogs, and posts from businesses every week. You need them to know your business is something special right away. You need to spark that sense of something special—something magical.

Or else, you might lose them.

SPEAK TO YOUR AUDIENCE

If you want to show them you are something special, you have to talk to them the way they talk. If Paul had gone to the agora of some Greek city and started speaking in Hebrew, quoting Leviticus, no one would have given him a second glance. Instead, he spoke Greek, and he spoke about the things that concerned them. That's why they were open to what he was selling.

You know your ideal customer.

How do they talk?

What do they watch?

What references speak to them?

What are they worried about?

What do they think is funny?

Speak to them through their humor, their concerns, their favorite references.

The shorts company Chubbies does this really well. They know that their customers are guys who enjoy having a good time, so they focus on talking about having fun on the weekend and getting out of the office. It's genius.

To do this authentically, you have to have an authentic relationship with people who are part of your ideal customer group. At The Brand Sunday, when we're working on content to speak to those young Christian women who make up our ideal customers, we make sure to talk to young Christian women first. We want to hear what they think about and talk about. If I just tried to wing this, it wouldn't come off well.

Refining the voice you're going to speak to your customers in can be quite tricky for those who aren't natural writers, so if you aren't great with your words, it may be worthwhile working with a copywriter for this.

START WITH YOUR WEBSITE

You have to make an authentic, quality first impression online that speaks directly to your ideal customer.

Eventually, you'll reach out through almost every channel you can online, but before you sign up for an account on everything from Facebook to Medium, you want to set up your own gathering place—your website.

Start by going to one of the reputable website template sites like Shopify or Wix or Squarespace or GoDaddy. One of the options they'll give you is to purchase a domain name. A domain name is essentially the web address that your customers will put into their browser to find you. This will cost a little extra, but it's absolutely worth it because you want your domain name to be easy to remember.

We all know the value of a great website address. It's far easier to remember to visit BestBostonBagels.com than FreeWebsite.com/BagelsBoston43103.

So choose something easy to remember that relates directly to your business name and/or what it does.

Domain in hand, pick a template that fits your aesthetics, polish the language you worked on for your story and core values, add some images that resonate with the people you want to reach, direct them where to buy, and click publish.

You want to do this first because the whole value of reaching out on social media is giving people *somewhere to go.*

Like my posts? Check out my site!

Like my designs? Go buy some here!

Think I'm funny? Find out more by following this link.

You can sell stuff without having a website, but the truth is, people just don't trust a company that doesn't have a website. It feels suspicious, not professional.

If a competitor has a website and you don't, they'll almost certainly get most of the business.

But don't fret too much. You don't have to have a complicated website full of videos and animation. A good website can be as simple as a single page with one or two pictures and a few sections that clearly talk about your business in a simplified way. Don't overdo it.

Just state who you are, what you stand for, the problem you're solving, and how you are going to solve it. People will then know enough about you to decide if they want your solution or not.

The point isn't to create an artistic masterpiece in digital space; it's to give potential customers a place to go to find out about why they should come to you.

SOCIAL MEDIA

Once you have a place to send your customers, it's time to move into that modern agora, social media, to get their attention.

Now's the time to finally get that TikTok account you've been dying for!

We all are so entrenched in it now, it's hard to remember what an amazing invention social media is. Because of these sites, you can talk directly to your customers every single day. For free! It's completely changed the nature of advertising.

The key to success in this agora is content—but not just any content. You can't slap the same story, completely unchanged, on different platforms.

You have to create content that speaks to the culture, audience, and capabilities of each platform.

Let me show you what I mean.

A podcast is basically a long-form conversation. You pick an interesting topic and dig in for thirty minutes or an hour. That format won't work on TikTok, where people post videos of sixty seconds or less. Instagram is extremely visual, with a focus on photos, while Facebook is a bit more of a mix between photos and longer text, and Twitter is nearly all short text.

What's more, each platform speaks to a different group of people.

Facebook has an older audience than Instagram, which has an older audience than TikTok. Twitter tends to appeal to journalists and sports and political junkies, while Pinterest is there for the more artistic types. Meanwhile, LinkedIn hits the business crowd.

So you can't make one post and splatter it everywhere. It has to be unique.

...Sort of.

You can actually get one piece of content to stretch pretty far—if you're creative.

The trick is to adapt the content to the platform. So a quote that you post on Twitter can go on Instagram if you add a good image. A short video can play on TikTok, Instagram, Facebook, and even Twitter with more or less description. Just make sure you post it directly on that platform, instead of linking it from one platform to another.

If you record a podcast, turn the video on and put it on YouTube as well. Then cut the conversation up into segments and post the best bits on Instagram and TikTok. You can then share a link to the video across LinkedIn, Twitter, and Facebook. And for good measure, you can transcribe the conversation, clean it up, and turn it into a blog post on Medium.

If this feels like going overboard, it is—but overboard is exactly what you want to be doing. When you're making content, keep a "more not better" concept in mind. It's easy to spend all your time making one really cool video, but your company is better served by having sixty or seventy pretty good videos for customers to click through.

Over time, you want to build up a huge content library because thousands of photos, videos, and blog posts will let you speak to more customers and answer more of their questions.

And that's why you shouldn't worry too much at first about how many people are looking at your content or how often they're sharing it.

First impressions matter, but if you aren't impressing many people at first, don't sweat it.

In some ways, it's better to start off obscure. Everyone loves the idea of going viral, but if you do that too early—before you have enough content to keep people interested or a selection of products to buy—it'll all be a waste.

So focus on making as much decent content as you can as quickly as you can and spreading it across every agora on the internet. Over time, you'll gain interest, and all that interest will have a place to go.

MOVING INTEREST INTO SALES

Of course, the ultimate purpose of all this outreach is to get potential customers to notice you, have a great first impression, go to your website, and then...what?

Buy something from you, obviously.

Go see your Big Idea, buy into it, and spread the word to a thousand of their closest friends.

But how do you do that?

Going from a first impression to a sale actually takes a bit more than just a good podcast or a well-designed website. It takes a funnel—the most powerful sales tool of the twenty-first century.

14

Funneling in New Customers

It's amazing to think about all the inventors who have changed our lives that most of us have never heard of. Do you know who invented the indoor toilet? Or air conditioning? Or the skateboard?

So many inventors toil in obscurity while their inventions change history. Take Stanford Ovshinsky. I guarantee Stanford changed your life, and this is almost certainly the first time you've heard his name. Over the course of the twentieth century, Ovshinsky invented technologies that have given us flat-screen TVs, smartphones, solar panels, and electric cars. He's regularly compared to Edison.

Clearly, Edison had a better publicist.

Here's another inventor you've never heard of: Elias St. Elmo Lewis. Though you don't know his name either, you have definitely seen Lewis's work—because Lewis invented the marketing funnel. Any time you click a link on a Facebook ad or open an email from a company, you're taking part in his invention.

He's the godfather of online marketing.

Not bad for a guy born in 1898.

WHAT IS A FUNNEL?

Lewis's great innovation was to realize there are four separate stages of a customer's journey: awareness, interest, desire, and action.

You find out about something.

You develop an interest in it.

You decide you want it.

And you buy it.

A marketer's job is to catch you early in that process and "funnel" you into buying a particular product from a particular company.

To do this, marketers use two main funnel types: direct response and nurture. With direct response, they capture someone ready to buy today. With nurture funnels, they slowly convince the person to purchase over time.

If you're online at all, you almost certainly encounter both every day. Any time you see an Instagram ad that is selling you some great shirt or offers you a discount if you order now, that's direct response. Any time you sign up for emails from a company that sends you interesting fashion advice or recipes every week, that's a nurture campaign.

That's not to say direct response is only on social media. You can definitely start a nurture campaign through an ad or send direct response funnels through emails. If you ever get those "20 percent off our sweaters only until December 31!" messages in your inbox, you know what I'm talking about.

The key difference is less *where* the funnel starts than *what* it's doing. A nurture campaign is trying to sell to you over a long period, and direct response wants your sale now.

Another difference between these funnels is that a nurture funnel usually requires a lead generator. This is something you give the person in exchange for their email and the chance to slowly funnel them toward a sale.

People don't want to let go of their email addresses. To get that info, you have to give them something they value.

This might be a PDF that shows how to grow a business from $0 to $10 million in twenty-four months. It could be access to a video series you've done. You might offer worksheets for homeschooling parents, info on the best companies to repaint houses, or a way to clean up carpet stains without expensive products.

At The Brand Sunday, we give away the first five chapters of *The Bible Study* for free. Send over your email, and we'll send you the chapters in a PDF instantly.

You might wonder why you'd bother with a nurture campaign. After all, isn't it better to just get people to buy today and get it over with?

...Sometimes.

Like most companies, we do tons of direct response marketing, and it's very effective—but not everybody is ready to buy right now. If you're selling something that's a bit expensive or that takes a little effort to try—like a drive across town to try the new Italian restaurant—a nurture campaign allows you to build trust, show authority, and engage regularly until the customer slowly comes to see you are worth that extra cost or effort.

And when you're about to launch a business, that's basically exactly what you have to do: convince a lot of people you are worth a try.

NURTURE CAMPAIGN BASICS

Starting to nurture potential customers way before you launch helps ensure people are interested when your doors open. You can build up all the trust and authority you need even as you line up your team and build out your online presence.

To do this, though, you have to come up with a great lead generator that connects to your product. It should be something that fits in your customer's interests and relates to your business. A restaurant may give away recipes or samples in exchange for email addresses. A plant nursery could give away advice on creating a good gardening space or offer a small houseplant to people who visit the nursery for the first time.

Once you've built a list, nurture them with regular emails that also give similar value.

Sunday sends out emails on—you guessed it—Sundays. We call it Sunday Bible Study Basics. They include a three-minute video with one tip on studying the Bible or understanding your faith. It doesn't take much to put those together, but it allows people to get to know the company and me and feel more comfortable making a purchase down the line.

That's exactly what you want to cultivate with your nurture campaigns as well. Unlike the direct response marketing we'll cover in a moment, nurture campaigns let you build a relationship.

And relationships are important, even in sales.

DIRECT RESPONSE BASICS

Relationships are important, but at the end of the day, sales are what keep your business—your purpose—running. And direct response marketing plays a huge role in bringing in those sales. How big? Well, let me ask you:

How much of a startup's success comes down to the product, and how much comes down to marketing?

The answer is shocking.

Marketing is by far the bigger factor.

You could have the best tamales in the state—in the country, on the whole planet—and if nobody's heard about it, nobody's coming in to try one.

And the best way to market to anyone today is through direct response social media ads. With these ads, you can get right in front of millions of potential customers and tell them exactly why your company is so awesome.

The big players you need to know about are Google and Facebook. Google ads don't just go on searches, they also go on websites you visit and on YouTube. Facebook ads can also go on Instagram. There are also LinkedIn ads, Twitter ads, Pinterest ads, TikTok ads, and so on. Basically every social media platform will have a way to advertise.

These ads don't work like your old-school billboard or newspaper ad. When you know how to do this right, you can target your ads to the exact people most likely to buy your stuff. You can get in front of every one of your ideal customers in your entire city—or even across the world. If you want to target every thirty-year-old nature lover with little kids who needs a new pair of jeans, social media direct response ads can do that for you.

Of course, these tools will continue to evolve over time. We may see data privacy laws enacted that change how we target customers, but one thing is sure to remain the same—and I'm not exaggerating when I say this:

It is the most powerful tool you have to build sales.

This is an investment. You might have to spend twenty dollars on marketing to garner a forty-dollar purchase. But so long as they spend the forty dollars now and come back to spend another forty dollars later, it's well worth the investment.

START THE COUNTDOWN

With a strong team in place, a significant online presence for your new customers to interact with, and a combination of nurture and direct response marketing funnels at work, you're finally—finally!—ready to take that big step.

It's time to launch your business and start living your purpose.

But before you fling the doors open, you want to blitz the market so that you can get the absolute most interest and business from your opening.

A big opening goes a long way toward long-term success. So now that you're ready to launch, it's time to put those final steps in place.

15

Ready to Launch

Even if you knew nothing about launches before this book, I bet you still have one envisioned in your head from a successful launch week.

It's an image of a man in a black turtleneck, standing on a stage, holding a phone.

That's the first iPhone you're thinking of, and the man is Steve Jobs. And that launch changed the world.

Of course, not every launch is so historical, but they each, in their way, can transform a purpose into a reality.

That was certainly true with *The Bible Study*. We launched through Kickstarter, and because we stuck the landing, we ended up with $24,000 within thirty days that allowed us to build the business into what it is today.

It's no exaggeration to say that launch changed my life.

And if you get this right, your launch can change yours.

CHOOSING A LAUNCH DATE

Thousands of businesses are launched every day. Most of those fail. We are overrun with ads everywhere we turn. We ignore most of them. If you want to stand out, you have to dedicate a lot of time to getting this launch right. And that actually starts not with a social media ad or a big ribbon-cutting ceremony but with a date on the calendar.

Every kind of business has a best season.

A toy company does best around Christmas time. A swimsuit company sells most of their product in late spring. To give yourself the best launch, you need to open in your best season. If you want to open a hot chocolate hotspot in Minnesota, you'll have a far better launch if you wait for the weather to get chilly. If you are selling custom kites, you will do better when the weather turns breezy and warm in spring.

But it's not quite as simple as that.

You don't want to launch right at the peak of interest. You want to launch a bit before.

Open that hot chocolate place in October when the weather is cooling but not frosty yet. That'll give you time for word of mouth to pick up and to make sure you have enough people working behind the counter. Start selling kites in March to catch those cool, bright days of early spring so you can have designs perfect for May and the summer ahead.

At The Brand Sunday, we never launch in the first quarter of the new year because everyone is still in the post-Christmas spending doldrums when they are trying to avoid unnecessary purchases. Instead, we launch right around August—just in time for the school year. This gives us the advantage of being able to make necessary changes and work out the kinks in a product before the big sales season that kicks off on Black Friday.

There's an ideal time to launch every Big Idea, from a self-help book to a grain-free dog food company. Search Google, and you'll find that almost every kind of business is busier at one time of year or another.

Once you know when the optimal time is to launch, count back a couple months. That's how long you need to get all your launch materials in order. If you're launching in August, you want to be working on this in June.

So pick your launch date, mark that time on your calendar, make sure you have enough time to prepare, and start counting down to launch.

PREPARING TO LAUNCH

The date's on the calendar, now it's time to roll up your sleeves and get to work on that pre-launch preparation. This is going to be an all-out effort that covers the entire week before you open, so you've got to have everything lined up.

That way, all you have to do is hit Launch and watch your business take off.

Deals

How often have you passed the same jacket ten times only to finally give in and buy it? What made the difference that eleventh time?

Odds are it was the discount.

A discount is a pretty powerful incentive. Feeling like you're getting a deal makes it far more tempting to take a chance on something. That's why setting your discounts on your Big Idea is the place to start in your launch week prep.

If you've done your pricing right, there's a decent amount of room in your price for an attractive discount that you run one week only, while supplies last, without losing money on your sales.

20 percent off

Buy one, get one free

Free shipping

Whatever you can afford to offer to get people in the door or on the site, this is the time to do it.

Discounts are only one type of deal in your toolbox, though. You can also offer various upselling deals. An upsell is when you try to convince customers to buy more than one item from you through a good deal. You can do this through many different tactics:

Bumps add a small product after your customer chooses their big purchase, like adding fries to your burger meal.

Bundles bring multiple products together at a special price, like getting five razor blades, shaving cream, and aftershave for the price of just the razors.

And subscriptions allow your customers to repeat their purchase indefinitely, like receiving your favorite tea every month in the mail.

Upsells are useful because they end up making you more profit while the customer feels like they got a deal. Those fries McDonald's sells you cost almost nothing but earn them an extra dollar in profits off the bump to the meal. That razor blade bundle convinces you to pay for five blades when you only wanted two.

To get this boost in revenue, you don't need to invent a whole bunch of new Big Idea products, you just need to be creative with some extras.

For instance, a bakery can bump a donut into a breakfast with a cup of coffee at a nice markup. A clothing shop can simply bundle multiple versions of the same shirt in different colors. At The Brand Sunday, we offer multiple bundles like the Best Life Bundle, which includes *The Bible Study* and *The Best Season Planner* for a discounted price. We also offer the option to get digital versions for a little more.

There's really no end to how you do this. The end result should simply be that you offer customers a nice assortment of deals to choose from during launch week that makes them feel like they really need to give your Big Idea a try now.

Get the Word Out

Deals firmly in place, you need to make sure as many people as possible hear about you, your business, and the amazing pre-launch deals you're offering. This is an all-out campaign, so you'll want to use every last communication tool you have.

Start with your email list.

If you've run your nurture campaigns successfully, you now have a decent number of email addresses that you've been emailing regularly to keep their interest. Now is the time to push them to buy.

You can do that by writing up a series of emails to send during launch week that encourages them to make that first purchase.

The same schedule works for just about any company:

Day 1: Tell everyone you will be launching tomorrow and introduce your deals.

Day 2: Let them know that it's Launch Day! And that these deals will only last for five more days.

Day 3: Share answers to any big questions. You can guess what these will be beforehand and write this before like all the rest of your emails. For instance, I knew from talking to friends there'd be questions about which Bible translation we used. I answered that in the email.

Day 4: Take the day off.

Day 5: Share how grateful you are for the response you've been getting and how great things are going.

Day 6: Remind everyone there's only one day left. If you have a physical product, tell them there's only a limited quantity left.

Day 7: Email in the morning and evening to remind everyone that this is the last day to get the deals before your official launch and build some urgency.

These email messages may seem a little obvious, but trust me, the old marketing tricks work. People love a good deal, and if you keep reminding them they only have a little time to get it, they will inevitably jump on board.

Spread the word through your social media accounts.

The aim here is to make sure people learn about your deals while avoiding being *too* persistent. You want to remind them consistently, but you don't want to annoy them. I recommend posting up to two times per day per platform for the entire launch week. Try to have some variety in the posts so they don't get redundant. Talk about your business and product from different sincere, practical, and amusing angles.

And make sure all your friends, family, and church community help spread the word by liking and sharing everything you post.

Email and social media are the two best channels you have to speak to people in the time leading up to your launch. But there are potentially other ways to generate some attention.

And perhaps the best is generating some free press. You can set up interviews with local media—TV, newspapers, magazines—and online through podcasts or blogs.

This is a great way to introduce yourself, your business, and your Big Idea to a wider audience, and since people in the media are always looking for content, the benefit is mutual.

Try to tailor your interviews to your ideal customers or your local area. You only have so much time, and you want to get in front of as many potential ideal customers as you can.

Spend a Little Money

Everything I've recommended for launch week has been totally free up to this point. However, your best tool to achieve a successful launch is going to cost you something.

Your Number One, best launch tool is social media ads. And those will cost some money.

Whether you want to get customers to visit a physical location or only your website, online ads are the best way to generate customer interest. Hopefully, you've already been running some of these to set up nurture campaigns and spur some early interest.

Whether you have or not, though, now is the time to go all in online.

You want ads up across the major online ad platforms of Facebook/Instagram and Google/YouTube. Just like with your social media posts, you'll want some variety here. You can run unboxing ads and problem-solving ads. You can do lifestyle shoots and work with influencers to post about your business.

Make sure all of these speak to your ideal customer, though. If you use influencers, their ideal customers should also be your ideal customers.

And, if you can afford it, this is the moment to bring in an outside marketing organization to help you get these ads right.

WHAT COMES NEXT

If you do all of this, hopefully your launch day brings in enough revenue to fuel your business on its way to great heights.

Even though you've probably worked harder on this than anything in your life, this is no time to take a vacation. Once people get a load of your Big Idea, you have to start the hard work of convincing them to buy again—and again, and again, and again—while also getting their friends to buy as well. You need to build off your positive feedback by sharing reviews on social media or even putting them into a social media ad. You need to start a new nurture campaign through your now more extensive email list. You need to get back in touch with those podcasts and local media channels to share how well you did and see if they want to make that a story.

And while you're at it, you need to work out whatever kinks you've discovered in your process so that when the next big sale opportunity hits, you're ready for even bigger numbers.

Living your purpose through a business that matters can be almost all-absorbing, and the months and years ahead will be full of challenges. That's why, now that you've launched out to sea, you need to focus on charting a course toward success, not for one week, but for years to come.

16

Setting a Course for Success

We had plans for a huge Q4 in 2020 at The Brand Sunday. Early in the year, we had put in a massive order for *The Bible Study*. In Q1, all signs were that we were trending toward an incredibly good year, and we wanted to make sure we had plenty of supply.

Then COVID happened.

That actually went okay for us because people were at home and eager for a way to connect with God.

Then the election became the most expensive in history—pricing us out of a lot of ads. And that didn't go so well for us.

Luckily, we were able to shift priorities. As soon as we knew how serious the crisis would be, we set to work making slow but steady progress toward a solution. We put off buying more product stock until early 2021, cutting our expenses. We also set up opportunities for customers to purchase some products at wholesale price and others in well-priced bundles to encourage thrifty customers to still buy *something* for friends at Christmas. That left us with more room to store the extra copies of *The Bible Study* we still had lying around.

Because we were adaptable, we got through this unprecedented crisis.

I hope you never have to face a crisis this unexpected and this serious as a business owner, but you always have to be ready for it. No matter how hard you try, you will never know what is ahead next quarter or next year. All you can do is set a course for success and take those slow steps toward it.

SUCCESS TAKES DISCIPLINE

Now that you've launched your Big Idea, it's time to make sure we've gone and burst a few fantasy bubbles—in particular, the fantasy of overnight success. A lot of entrepreneurs, once they get through all the tough work we've covered in this part and officially launch their business, expect to make a bunch of money overnight. They start planning how they'll spend their first million before they've done a thousand in sales.

So I just want to remind you of one thing:

This is going to take a while.

And it's going to take a lot of work.

A successful launch is wonderful. It's the best start imaginable! But there are probably years ahead of you in which you have to keep focused on your purpose with every minute you have.

The fact is, even the best businesspeople in the world work at their purpose *for years* before they see real success. Twenty-seven years old is the average age at which someone starts on their journey to their first million, and they don't usually achieve it until thirty-five. On average, then, there are eight years of backbreaking work between a Big Idea and the big payday.

Across the board, even the most brilliant businesspeople of our time had to work for years to achieve success:

It took Bill Gates six years.

Warren Buffet took five years.

Michael Bloomberg took seven years.

Phil Knight took sixteen years.

Even Jeff Bezos had to wait three years.

What I'm saying is that there are very few truly overnight successes in this world. To succeed takes time—and it takes a plan.

Business is brutal. The vast majority of entrepreneurs are far more likely to fail in six months than make a million dollars. Those who manage to keep their business afloat face years before they can establish steady revenue, let alone putting a million dollars in their bank account.

I know the work you've already done has been difficult. It's going to get even harder now. Business requires a lot of sacrifice. I was paying sixteen people for quite some time before I paid myself a dollar.

To get from business planning to business success takes discipline and a focus on taking each step, one at a time, until you can start reaping the rewards of what you've sown.

SET A COURSE OF SMALL STEPS

The entrepreneur Jim Rohn once said, "Success is nothing more than a few disciplines practiced every day."

Rohn is right. The success of your business probably won't come down to big, bold Hollywood moments—showdowns in the boardroom or landing that one big client. It'll come down to the small steps you took every day that slowly led you in the right direction. Even if you end up in that boardroom, it'll be those small steps that brought you there.

So getting the small steps right is critical.

That's what James Clear's book *Atomic Habits* is all about. As Clear put it, "A goal is a desired outcome. A strategy is a desired outcome combined with a plan for achieving it. Create strategies, not goals."

I don't think he means you shouldn't have goals. It's more that you should focus on the step-by-step strategies that lead where you want to go. Even though you are now working on a real business with real products and real customers, you still have to focus on that time management and chipping away at whatever is holding your company back.

The problems will be different, but the strategy is the same. You may now have all the details of your Big Idea worked out and have a logo and a story ready to win over customers. But new issues will come with your newly opened doors.

How do you manage a business after launch?

What is the one position you need filled by an expert?

How do you grow your brand from your launch?

What do you do with your first complaints?

When do you start introducing your next Big Idea to the business?

Building on early success requires answering questions like these every day. And that can be incredibly, frustratingly daunting. You want to take launch and shoot off like a rocket to the stars. Instead, you're stuck floating in orbit, tinkering with the controls, and trying to learn how to pilot this big, complex machine as you go.

That's why the same advice you've followed up until now has to remain in place. Continue to set aside that hour or so every day to solve each of these problems in turn.

After the shop is closed, after the last order is filled, after the final customer is satisfied for the day, close up and work away at each problem as it arises.

And remember, as you go forward, to leave room for God to open doors. Don't become impatient for a chance to jump ahead or become too wed to one idea. God opens doors, but those aren't always the doors you expect, nor are they usually set to your schedule.

But that doesn't mean He isn't working for your success. God blesses obedience and hard work. When you demonstrate faith and a willingness to dig in against adversity, He responds in absolutely incredible ways.

I'm not exaggerating here.

The only reason that I ever saw success was because God was invested in that success. I attribute all of it to Him.

Remember, Proverbs 19:21 tells us:

"Many are the plans in the mind of a man,

but it is the purpose of the Lord that will stand."

God knows where you are going. Let Him lead, and just keep taking one step after another—through the big triumphs and the big setbacks—all the way to your purpose.

STAY THE COURSE

Not every launch leads to a boom in business. Not every Big Idea becomes profitable. Not every business stays open. The COVID pandemic closed more than one hundred thousand businesses in America. Plenty of those belonged to Christian entrepreneurs trying to do work that means something.

So while it's important to set out on a clear course as you prepare to launch and to keep moving forward once you do, there will always be a question at the back of every entrepreneur's mind:

When is it time to give up and go back to the drawing board?

My answer: later.

That's not to say there isn't a time to walk away and try something new. But most people are too eager to fail. They read a setback as a sign their idea is doomed and try to back out. Simply hanging on and working away at those small steps is often enough to overcome a setback.

Companies from FedEx to Airbnb also faced major crises that could have led to failure—only to rally and become world-changing brands.

There may come a moment when you have faced so many setbacks that you have to redirect your dream. After all, it took me four failures before I built a business that took off. I had to walk away from those businesses in order to open the door to this one.

Making the choice to call it a day is a personal one, and only you can know when enough has been enough. Just make sure it's truly the end and not a new beginning when you shut that door.

SETTING COURSE FOR SUCCESS AHEAD

There are many hard days ahead, many long nights, and many tough calls—but with God in partnership, your success will come.

Someday, you'll wake up and realize you don't have to go into work that day because things are running well on their own. You won't worry over the numbers in the accounts because business will be solid.

...But then what do you do?

What do you do once you've actually built a truly successful business?

You expand your purpose.

Part V

Living with Purpose

17

Where a Business That Matters Can Lead You

Blake Mycoskie, the founder of TOMS Shoes, came up with his Big Idea on a trip to Argentina. He saw these shoes called alpargatas that were great looking, comfortable, and cheap to manufacture. For some reason, Americans had never caught on to this trend in footwear, so Mycoskie decided he would be the one to introduce those shoes to the American market. When he got back to the States, he worked with designers to create a pair he could mass produce.

The company blew up.

That sounds like a pretty standard business success story, but there's one difference: Mycoskie didn't found TOMS in order to get rich; he did it to do something that mattered. The reason he wanted to make alpargatas popular was so he could finance his dream to give shoes away to the children he saw walking around Argentina barefoot.

TOMS was the best way he could achieve that purpose. People would buy a pair of shoes for themselves, and Mycoskie would take some of the profit from the sale and make another pair to give away to a child in need.

Mycoskie came up with a system in which everyone wins. All because he approached business not just from a perspective of making money, but of doing something that matters.

MONEY AND—BUSINESS

Mycoskie found his God-given purpose in creating TOMS, and I hope you've done the same through the pages of this book. And like Mycoskie, I hope your purpose is bigger than just achieving big sales.

What makes you different from the other entrepreneurs out there is that you work for the Kingdom.

I know I've told you that before—at length—but it's easy to lose focus on that point as a business goes from a concept to a reality with real revenue, real customers, and real employees. The temptation to cut back on what makes your company matter in order to finance a second store or pay back a bank loan is enormous.

I can help the homeless next year. We're running a little behind now.

If I just cut back on the fair trade items, we could really blow up.

Giving everyone a raise would make the budget tight. Better to wait until sales pick up.

As your business develops, it's critical you don't give in to these thoughts and lose focus on why you are partnering with God in your purpose. The whole reason to do this is to improve lives and make the world better.

Living up to that responsibility is the only definition of success that matters here.

When you're working with God, success doesn't come with a dollar amount. Not every business makes millions, and your path to that kind of income may be long—or it may never come. But if you continue to put God first and prioritize the positive ways you can make your business matter, you are a great success, however much you have in your pocket.

That's not to say money doesn't matter, but you should approach business from a "money and—" perspective.

Money and—charity.

Money and—testifying to God's love.

Money and—a place where employees are treated and paid well.

Money and—environmentalism.

Paul never became rich building tents. Jesus never made much as a carpenter. But their purpose was so grand, no one would ever think of them as anything but rich.

Which is just what Jesus said!

> *"Do not lay up for yourselves treasures on earth, where moth and rust destroy and where thieves break in and steal, but lay up for yourselves trea-sures in heaven, where neither moth nor rust destroys and where thieves do not break in and steal. For where your treasure is, there your heart will be also."*

Matt. 6:19–21

REDEFINING SUCCESS

I've talked a lot about businesses that are models for how to matter as a Christian entrepreneur. Whether it's Charity: Water, Warby Parker, or Chick-fil-A, each company finds a way to do God's work and participate in God's story—whether they are explicit or even conscious about it or not.

By following this path, you join them. Perhaps your contribution will be smaller in terms of dollars or individuals reached—perhaps it will be much greater!—but by being part of God's story, we are all on an even footing before Him.

This is true even if your business fails. Even if it never makes you a cent.

God's idea of success is so much grander than money. You may enter into business as a musician and never be able to work at it full-time. But by providing that joy to others and finding a way to make that music matter, you are as great a success as Bill Gates.

I failed at business four times. There was a moment, in that Starbucks parking lot, when I thought I *was* a failure.

And at that moment, that was true, not because my business ideas had struggled to take off but because I wasn't in partnership with God in my plans. I had failed Him because I put dollars before Him. Even if *The Bible Study* had never become a publishing success, it would have made *me* a success anyway because it brought me back to Him.

That's how I know that every person reading this can be a success, too. I don't know how much money your Big Idea can make or what the future holds for your business. But if you work with God to make something that matters, you're the most successful businessperson on the planet.

THIS DOESN'T HAVE TO BE PAINFUL

I don't want you to walk away from this thinking that building a business that matters puts you at a disadvantage or makes it more likely for you to fail in a practical sense. Far from it.

Every business I've mentioned in this book is wildly successful. They are all profitable. The owners are all doing fine. Blake Mycoskie is doing very well for himself. So are the owners of Warby Parker and Chick-fil-A.

Living purpose through a business that matters is good business.

Shaquille O'Neal has said that he learned how to invest from Jeff Bezos. The lesson he learned? Make investments "based on if it's going to change people's lives." He claimed he'd quadrupled his worth since he started following that advice.

The truth is, doing the work of the Kingdom doesn't have to be painful. You don't have to give away every dollar that comes in. A world of good is done by giving away just 1 percent.

Donating extra food before it goes off at your restaurant feeds your community, even as it probably saves you money. Paying someone an extra dollar may only raise the price of your coffee by a penny, but you may have kept that person in a home.

That's the blessing of following this path. And that's why I'm so excited to be on it with you.

18

Living Out Your God-Given Purpose

In 2020, billionaire Chuck Feeney died having achieved his greatest wish: he gave away every cent he had. As we have seen recently, many of the world's wealthiest people have also pledged to do the same thing.

Here's another story. A while back, I was sitting in Spoon & Stable, with my wife and my friends Tiago, Ethan, and Allie. I was feeling super content. We were laughing nonstop, enjoying great food, and I was overjoyed being with people I loved.

It was an ordinary moment that seemed extraordinary, and I realized something:

I wanted more of those.

And so I decided I'd work fewer hours. I wanted more time with Gisela and more time with friends. I offloaded a lot of my responsibilities, and I made it a priority to make time for what really mattered.

PURPOSE BEYOND BUSINESS

What do those stories have in common?

In each one, someone realized they were more than their business.

For Chuck Feeney and the other billionaire philanthropists, it was about realizing that they were more than the money they'd made. For me, it was about realizing there was more to my life than long hours trying to help my business succeed.

That revelation was huge for me, and a long time coming.

I've spent my whole adult life working nonstop. Literally nonstop. I spent years without a day off. I didn't really know what to do with myself if I wasn't working. I was a workaholic.

But Gisela, Miami, VOUS Church, friends, and family all started to make me reconsider that approach. Maybe I didn't need to put in those weekend hours *every* weekend. Maybe I could take a day off and just...be, like I was that night at Spoon & Stable.

The benefits were almost instantaneous. I started being more involved at VOUS. I was blown away by this huge group of young adults that were all chasing after the same thing—to love God and love others. The people were extremely encouraging—which can be hard to find in the church world as an entrepreneur for some reason. And, I may be biased, but we have the best pastor around.

Living life for Jesus was a cool thing, not something to be ashamed of. Focusing on helping people in my new community was a cool thing, not something to be put off.

At this point, I can't imagine ever going back to the 24/7/365 grind. I needed to achieve my purpose in business, but once I did, I realized there was more to my purpose than just a job.

WHO ARE YOU AFTER BUSINESS HOURS?

If you stick at this, with God's help, you will eventually be in a position to work less. You can hire more people to fill in on some of your responsibilities. You can take a breath and a step back.

...And do what?

What will you do with that free time when it arrives? Where do you want to put your energy, time, and passion?

For me, it was family and friends. I'd lost a lot of connections while pursuing business success, and I was ready to take that time to enjoy the love that was in my life. For you, it could be any number of things. Perhaps it's expressing yourself in art or getting into great physical shape. Perhaps it's starting on that next Big Idea that you put aside at first.

Or perhaps it's finding a way to give even more than your business is giving.

If you're young, you may not realize that Bill Gates used to be rich and famous for something other than giving money away. When I was young, Bill Gates was something of a villain. He was the head of Microsoft and seemed remote and duplicitous. Sure, he'd given the world Windows and Office, but he just seemed to always be conniving something. What was he doing with all that money and power?

But that was before he started giving billions away to fight diseases all around the world.

These days, Gates is known far more for the good he's done with his money than how he got it. He became a success in business; then he became bigger than success.

If you're doing good through your business, that doesn't mean you can't do even more on your own. If your business gives away 1 percent of its profits, you can donate another 10 percent from your salary.

Wherever your business takes you, never forget to put God first in all your choices—professional and personal. Let Him guide you where you can be most useful to Him. And always ask yourself what value you can add to the world with each choice.

VALUE YOURSELF

Life can't just be about helping others. You also have to take care of yourself. Working fourteen-hour days, grinding through every last task you can finish, can't go on forever. You're going to burn out, and you're going to feel unfulfilled even when you're living your purpose.

There's nothing to be proud of in sleeping four hours a night and never seeing your family. Unless you're saving lives and can't ever get away, it's going to end up doing more harm than good.

There's so much to do to launch a business that matters— it's so easy to feel overwhelmed—it's important to recognize the value in taking care of yourself.

Instead of being in a rush to hit some artificial valuation of your business, treasure your time. If it takes six months to open, that's okay. If it takes six years, that's okay too. If you are working within your purpose and partnering with God on something that matters, that time is well-spent, and it's okay to block off time for yourself.

If we want to live and love like Jesus wants us to, we need to be spiritually, physically, and mentally fit. And that requires us to take time for the small things—studying Scripture, listening to music, and praying but also drinking really good coffee, getting some sleep, and having a lazy morning with our family.

Fill your cup because that's the only way it can overflow into the lives of others.

To do that, you may have to learn how to say no to things that seem really interesting or exciting or may advance your business in some way. Give yourself permission to turn down good opportunities when the timing isn't right. And don't regret it later.

Tend to your cup. Because if it's running empty, you don't have anything left for others.

And helping others, that's what really matters in the end.

Conclusion

I'm so excited to see where God takes you now. I can't wait to see the incredible Big Ideas that are about to hit the world.

At this point, I hope the way forward is clear. You have the steps to bring you closer to God's story, set yourself up for the obstacles ahead, and move point by point from concept to Big Idea to business launch. Most importantly, you have God to help you through this. His *rhema* will guide you to your God-given purpose and to a business that matters.

Most of all, though, I pray that the advice in this book helps you live the purpose God designed you for—with God and for all of us.

A Special Thanks

Gisela, everything I work on is for you. Everything.

Tony and Elsa, we can be roommates anytime. Dinner Tuesday?

Caleb Cruse for being there through the highs and lows.

Caleb Brose for clearing my plate so I can dream. You're a Godsend.

Bree Graham for giving me my sanity back.

Katlyn Hovland for being the reason people love our stuff.

Paul Weaver for making me look way cooler than I am.

Brett and Sheila Waldman for your dedication and support. Who knew we would need so many fulfillment stations?

The Activ team: Antonio, Alex, Hannah, Daniel, Austin, Meg, for getting our books in front of so many eyes. Let's go to San Diego again.

Everyone at Scribe, especially Seth and Maggie, for turning my endless pages of notes and stories into this completed work. There's nobody like you guys.

Tiago Magro for inspiring me to work hard and love harder.

Ethan Salau for every conversation, especially over a meal. I'm happy we gave it a second chance.

Jesse Roberson for supporting *The Bible Study* when we just had fifty promo copies and we went to Kona every other day.

VOUS Church for being my home.

Jesus for saving me and demonstrating what it means to bring heaven to earth.

As I was writing these, I kept wanting to mention something about food in every one. So, I guess we should all go celebrate over dinner. I'm down if you're down. Either way, I love every one of you from the bottom of my heart.

About the Author

Author and entrepreneur Zach Windahl has helped thousands of people better understand the Bible and grow closer to God through his company, The Brand Sunday. He's the author of several books, including *The Bible Study*, *The Bible Study: Youth Edition*, and *The Best Season Planner*. Zach lives in Miami, Florida, with his wife, Gisela, and their dog, Nyla.

CPSIA information can be obtained
at www.ICGtesting.com
Printed in the USA
LVHW111041060822
725339LV00019B/397